LOST IN TRANSLATION: EFFECTIVE LEGAL WRITING FOR THE INTERNATIONAL LEGAL COMMUNITY

LexisNexis Law School Publishing Advisory Board

LOST IN TRANSLATION: EFFECTIVE LEGAL WRITING FOR THE INTERNATIONAL LEGAL COMMUNITY

Kevin J. Fandl
Adjunct Professor of Law
Georgetown University Law Center

LexisNexis®

ISBN: 978–0–7698–5746–6 (print)
ISBN: 978–0–3271–7982–5 (eBook)

Library of Congress Cataloging-in-Publication Data

Fandl, Kevin J.
Lost in translation : effective legal writing for the international legal community / Kevin J. Fandl, J.D., Ph.D.
pages cm
Includes index.
ISBN 978-0-7698-5746-6 (perfect bound)
1. Legal composition. 2. Law--Language. I. Title.
K94.F36 2013
808.06'634--dc23
2013006398

NOTE TO USERS
To ensure that you are using the latest materials available in this area, please be sure to periodically check the LexisNexis Law School web site for downloadable updates and supplements at www.lexisnexis.com/lawschool.

Editorial Offices
121 Chanlon Rd., New Providence, NJ 07974 (908) 464-6800
201 Mission St., San Francisco, CA 94105-1831 (415) 908-3200
www.lexisnexis.com

MATTHEW BENDER

(2013–Pub.3374)

Dedication

For my wife, Monica, who understands and supports my dreams, no matter how high in the clouds I go. And for my daughter, Isabella, who fills my heart with happiness and peace with every smile. Thank you both for your patience and love.

Acknowledgment

I owe a special thanks to Amy McQuade for her keen eye and diligent work as an editor for this text. Amy was essential in making this book a useful tool for legal practitioners everywhere. Effective legal writing is never achieved alone.

About the Author

Dr. Kevin J. Fandl is a legal writing scholar with extensive publishing and teaching experience. He served as a managing editor for the Foreign Policy Bulletin for three years and as a senior editor on the American University International Law Review for two years. He has published ten law review articles, several editorials and book reviews, and recently published a text on Legal English for foreign legal practitioners (ABA, 2012). He is the director of the Global Legal Education Institute, which develops and delivers on-site professional development training and legal writing consulting around the world on numerous U.S. law topics. Dr. Fandl earned his Master's degree in International Relations and his Juris Doctor degree in Law from American University and his Doctorate in Public Policy from George Mason University. He lectures frequently at Georgetown University Law Center and the American University Washington College of Law, and consults occasionally for the World Bank and the Organization of American States.

Introduction

A globalized law market necessarily implies cross-border legal communications. Whether it is a non-U.S. attorney providing legal guidance to a U.S. firm, or a U.S. client located overseas receiving that advice directly, there is a rapidly growing need for foreign legal practitioners to communicate their legal ideas in English. It is essential that their advice be communicated effectively in English so as to maintain the meaning of the words and to properly counsel their partner or client. Mistakes in translation, grammar, style, and form may not only misconstrue the advice — it can lead to unwanted actions and even frustration of the guidance. This book was developed with foreign legal practitioners and law students in mind, and focuses on providing clear solutions to common errors present in their legal writing. It is designed in an accessible format with samples of legal correspondence, contracts, academic abstracts, and citations to allow the reader to obtain quick answers to their drafting questions.

Table of Contents

Chapter 1 INTRODUCTION **1**

Chapter 2 THE IMPORTANCE OF EFFECTIVE LEGAL WRITING FOR FOREIGN LEGAL PRACTITIONERS **5**

[A] WHAT ARE THE RISKS OF INEFFECTIVE LEGAL WRITING? 7
[B] WHAT MAKES AMERICAN LEGAL WRITING UNIQUE? 8
[1] Demand for Brevity 8
[2] Plain Legal English 9
[3] Clear Issue Identification 10
[4] Succinct Conclusions 11
[C] LEGAL DOCUMENTS: AN OVERVIEW 12

Chapter 3 MAKING YOUR WRITING EFFECTIVE **15**

[A] INTRODUCTION 15
[B] WORD CHOICE 15
[C] SUPERFLUOUS LANGUAGE 17
Exercise: Superfluous Language 18
[D] SENTENCE STRUCTURE 19
[E] CLEAR SENTENCES 20
[F] TRANSITIONS 20
[G] SENTENCE SEQUENCING AND PARAGRAPH STRUCTURE 21
[H] AMBIGUOUS DRAFTING AND WORD CHOICE 21
Exercise: Drafting to Avoid Ambiguity 22
[I] PARALLEL STRUCTURE 23
Exercise — Parallel Structure 23
[J] VOICE 24
Exercise: Active/ Passive Voice 24
[K] REVIEW: LEGAL STYLE 25
[L] A FEW FINAL POINTERS 26
[1] Punctuation 26
[2] Spacing 26
[3] Capitalization 27
[4] Acronyms 27

Chapter 4 DRAFTING CORRESPONDENCE 29

[A] INTRODUCTION 29
[B] GENERAL CORRESPONDENCE 29
[C] CLIENT ADVICE LETTER 30
Exercise: Edit and Rewrite the Following Demand Letter 31
[D] EMAIL COMMUNICATIONS 32
Exercise: Email Correspondence 33
[E] TECHNOLOGY TIPS 34
[1] Delaying Message Delivery 34
[2] Requesting Return Receipt or Read Notification 35
[3] Setting Custom Auto-Signatures for Different Types of Correspondence . . 36
[F] A FEW CLOSING THOUGHTS ON TECHNOLOGY IN THE LEGAL PROFESSION 39

Chapter 5 DRAFTING LEGAL MEMORANDA AND CASE BRIEFS 41

[A] INTRODUCTION 41
[B] THE LEGAL MEMORANDUM 41
[1] Headings 42
[2] Question Presented 42
[3] Short Answer 43
[4] Statement of the Facts 44
[5] Discussion 44
[6] Conclusion/Recommendations 47
Exercise, Part 1: Framing the Issue 48
Exercise, Part 2: Applying Sources of Law 49
[C] CLOSING THOUGHTS ON LEGAL MEMORANDA 50
[D] CASE BRIEFS 51
[1] Parties/Case Citation 52
[2] Facts/Procedural History 53
[3] Issues 53
[4] Decision/Holding 53
[5] Reasoning 54
[6] Separate Opinions 54
[7] Analysis 54

Chapter 6 DRAFTING CONTRACTS 57

[A] INTRODUCTION 57
[B] THE IMPORTANCE OF EFFECTIVE CONTRACT DRAFTING SKILLS 57

[C] LETTERS OF INTENT 58
[D] TYPES OF CONTRACT LANGUAGE 59
[1] Language of Obligation/Discretion 60
[E] THE FRONT OF THE CONTRACT 62
[1] Contract Title and Introductory Clause 62
[2] Recitals 63
[F] THE BODY OF THE CONTRACT 64
[1] Defined Terms 64
Exercise: Defined Terms 64
[2] The Choice of Law/Forum Clause 65
[a] *Choice of Law Clause* 65
[b] *Choice of Forum* 66
[c] Forum Non Conveniens 66
[3] The Representations and Warranties Clause 67
[4] The Disclaimer Clause 68
[5] The Indemnification Clause 68
[6] The Merger Clause 69
[7] The Liquidated Damages Clause 69
[8] The Term and Termination Clause 70
[9] Severability/Saving Clause 70
[10] The Notice Clause 71
[11] Force Majeure Clause 71
[12] Waiver Clause 72
[13] Counterparts 72
[14] Boilerplate Clauses 73
[G] THE BACK OF THE CONTRACT 73
[1] The Signature Page 73
[2] Attachments, Exhibits, and Schedules 74
[H] DRAFTING POINTERS 75
[1] Numbers and Currency 75
[2] Tips on Drafting Time of Day 75
[3] Tips on Drafting Currency 75
[4] Drafting Numbers 76
[I] WHY DO WE WANT A WRITTEN CONTRACT IN THE FIRST PLACE? 76
[J] PROMISSORY ESTOPPEL AND RELIANCE 79
[K] PAROL EVIDENCE 79

Chapter 7 ACADEMIC LEGAL WRITING 81

[A] INTRODUCTION 81
[B] TYPES OF ACADEMIC LEGAL WRITING 81
[1] Case Analyses 82
[2] Issue Papers 82
[C] STAGES OF ACADEMIC LEGAL WRITING 82
[1] Stage 1: Formulating a Research Topic 83
[a] *Finding a Topic* 84
[2] Stage 2: Turning Your Research Topic into a Research Question 85
[3] Stage 3: Outline Your Manuscript 87
[4] Stage 4: Develop and Execute a Research Plan 88
[5] Stage 5: Analyze Material with Original Writing 89
[6] Stage 6: Connect Thoughts with Transitions and Headings 89
[7] Stage 7: Validating Authorities 91
[8] Stage 8: Wrapping-Up the Article 91

Chapter 8 LEGAL CITATION 93

[A] INTRODUCTION 93
[B] THE IMPORTANCE OF LEGAL CITATION 93
[C] TECHNOLOGY AND CITATION 96

Chapter 9 EDITING AND FINALIZING YOUR DRAFT 99

[A] INTRODUCTION 99
[B] STEP 1: GRAMMAR AND STYLE EDITING 100
[C] STEP 2: SUBSTANTIVE EDITING 101
Exercise: Editing a Letter 103

Chapter 10 CONCLUDING POINTS 105

Appendix A: SOLUTIONS TO EXERCISES 107

[A] AMBIGUOUS DRAFTING EXERCISE 107
[B] SUPERFLUOUS LANGUAGE EXERCISE 108
[C] SENTENCE STRUCTURE EXERCISE 108
[D] PARALLEL STRUCTURE EXERCISE 109
[E] VOICE EXERCISE 109
[F] FRAMING THE ISSUE EXERCISE 109
Exercise 1: Client Johnson Issue Statement 109
Exercise 2: Client Lockett Issue Statement 111
[G] APPLYING SOURCES OF LAW EXERCISE 112

[H] EDITING A LETTER OF INTENT EXERCISE 114

Appendix B: SAMPLE DOCUMENTS 117

[A] SAMPLE OPINION LETTER 117
[B] SAMPLE DEMAND LETTER 119
[C] SAMPLE CASE BRIEF # 1 120
[D] SAMPLE CASE BRIEF #2 121
[E] SAMPLE OFFICE MEMORANDUM 123
[F] SAMPLE LETTER OF INTENT 128
[G] MODEL CORRESPONDENCE (LETTER) 130
[H] MODEL CORRESPONDENCE (EMAIL) 131
[I] SAMPLE DUE DILIGENCE REPORT 132

Appendix C: DICTIONARY OF SELECT LEGAL TERMS 135

Index I-1

Chapter 1

INTRODUCTION

A lawyer's greatest weapon is their words. These words can convince a jury of a defendant's innocence; persuade a major corporation to provide compensation to a disgruntled employee; or convince a policymaker to shift direction on proposed legislation. A lawyer has at his or her disposal a veritable armory of skills in the sciences of communication and persuasion and it is expected that he or she will apply those tools in appropriate situations.

The value of a lawyer's advice remains in his or her analysis and assessment of a particular situation. Their knowledge of the law, understanding of the legal structure in which the law operates, and ability to cogently apply that law to a particular situation, is unmatched among other professions. It is because of this ability that clients look to lawyers for counsel and rely on their recommendations in making major decisions in their lives.

In recent years, the geographic scope of this counsel has been expanding. Lawyers from all parts of the world have been called upon to provide advice and even participate directly in matters that stretch beyond their jurisdiction. It is not uncommon today for a lawyer in Bogotá, for instance, to provide legal insight into a case being tried in New York. As a result of rapid growth in multinational business practice, as well as other cross-border activities, the role of a lawyer has effectively globalized.

With this expansion of legal services to foreign jurisdictions comes a substantial risk that can place the entirety of a lawyer's careful analysis in jeopardy. The risk is that the message not be properly communicated. A few simple grammar mistakes and misplaced modifiers can mean a complete loss of extensive legal advice. Writing across borders in different languages other than your own native tongue requires attention to not only the message that you want to convey, but also the way in which it is being conveyed.

Providing legal advice in English when English is not your first language is riskier than doing the same with non-legal advice. As I mentioned earlier, the guidance provided by a legal professional is often relied upon with little inquiry or doubt, given the trust that clients and colleagues generally have for attorneys. However, when that message is concealed or misconstrued in poor translation or incorrect usage in English, the damage may be irreparable and potentially harmful to a client. This is why it is especially important in law for non-U.S. legal professionals to either apply very careful English writing skills, or to use a qualified legal translator. Because the latter option is often prohibitively expensive, this book will attempt to address some of the key areas where messages are lost in translation.

Consider this recent article from the China Daily News, which stated:

> Translation errors in key contract terms have been responsible for igniting disputes between Chinese and foreign companies, the Shanghai Maritime Court said on Thursday after reviewing archives in the past two years . . . . "Online research has become much less time-consuming but not necessarily trustworthy. Cross-checking and verification have become more important".[1]

Here are additional comments supporting more emphasis on legal writing:

- "Lawyers in practice are generally judged by the final product they produce: the written, negotiated text. Clearly, in my firm, the first thing new lawyers will be judged upon is their writing. The fastest way to get ahead as a new lawyer is to be an able writer. The fastest way to fail is to be a poor writer."[2]
- "The current economic conditions don't change what we want to see from recent law graduates, but they do make it more imperative that new associates hit the ground running, and operate efficiently and effectively from day one."[3]
- "Over the years, I've heard a pretty consistent refrain of 'writing needs to improve' or 'I had to require the entire document.' Constructing grammatically correct sentences is not the problem. Rather, the ability to organize facts and principles in a crisp, logical way is what's lacking in many newcomers to the firm."[4]
- The President of Legal Writing Pro, Ross Guberman, "recently surveyed law firm partners in selected major firms and asked, 'What are the three writing problems you see most often in associate work product?' These were the most popular answers, in order: Poor structure/rambling organization; Passive voice/awkward sentences/ambiguous clauses; Clutter/wordiness; Grammar/usage/proofreading/attention to detail; Ineffective use of authorities."[5]

This book is intended to provide the non-U.S. legal practitioner or law student with essential tools to help them improve their communication in English. It is written in a straightforward and concise manner so as to be a practical rather than a theoretical tool. It includes examples and exercises meant to hone these skills and also to give

---

[1] Zhou Wenting, *"Translation errors cause disputes over contract terms,"* China Daily, Mar. 3, 2012, *available at* http://www.chinadaily.com.cn/cndy/2012-03/23/content_14894822.htm (accessed Sept. 25, 2012).

[2] Bryn Vaaler, *Compositional Practice: A Comment on "A Liberal Education in Law,"* 1 J.ALWD 148, 149 (2002).

[3] Kate Montgomery & Neda Khatamee, *What Law Firms Want in New Recruits,* New York Law Journal, 11 (April 2009) (quoting a hiring partner at an AmLaw 100 firm).

[4] Kate Montgomery & Neda Khatamee, *What Law Firms Want in New Recruits,* New York Law Journal, 15 (April 2009) (quoting a bankruptcy chair of an AmLaw 100 firm).

[5] Marcia Pennington Shannon, *Helping Associates Improve Their Writing Skills*, Law Practice, vol. 24, no. 1, 60 (Jan. 2008) (noting that Ross Guberman conducts hundreds of writing programs a year for many of the nation's top law firms, governmental agencies and bar associations. Guberman, who is the president of Legal Writing Pro and a former practicing lawyer, holds degrees from Yale, the Sorbonne and the University of Chicago School of Law).

immediate answers to some of the most perplexing questions presented when writing legal documents in English.

The text begins by describing an overall theme for improving your legal writing in English. This short section explains the importance of effective legal writing and addresses some of the more general techniques for making it effective. We will explore issues such as sentence and paragraph structure, transitions, punctuation, gender and number consistency, and quotations and paraphrasing. All of these skills will contribute to the improvement of your comprehensive writing technique.

The following four chapters address a specific type of legal writing. We begin with a look at legal correspondence, which, for some, is the most common mechanism for communicating in English. We move on to legal memoranda, or formal legal documents, in the next chapter, where we learn techniques for preparing carefully structured and properly footnoted drafts. We consider contracts after that, spending some time examining their unique style and format. And we finish this theme with a look at academic legal writing or writing for publication.

The remainder of the book addresses crucial, but secondary issues. These include proper citation using the BlueBook for legal citation, and editing techniques, including the use of technology to improve drafts. All of that is followed by a brief conclusion pulling together what we've covered. With that, let's get started!

Chapter 2

THE IMPORTANCE OF EFFECTIVE LEGAL WRITING FOR FOREIGN LEGAL PRACTITIONERS

An idea is only as good as the words that convey it. Non-U.S. legal practitioners who engage in multinational practice, especially in the U.S., have mastered their own legal rules as well as those of at least one other jurisdiction. In their own language, they can effectively persuade and explain the most basic and exceedingly complex ideas to a range of audiences. Yet, when they resort to English as their second language, they run a high risk that their ideas will get lost in translation.

For some, legal writing is like all other writing — a mechanism to communicate an idea to someone. Yet, for effective legal writers, writing is much more than that. Depending on your audience, you may be writing to persuade someone to take a particular action that they otherwise would not take; you may be writing to recommend a strategy or decision that affects human lives or millions of dollars; or you may be writing to explain an opinion that someone will rely upon when arguing before a court. Your writing is not just communicating an idea — it is attempting to facilitate a certain outcome.

Ineffective legal writing will obscure your idea and may ultimately fail to facilitate the outcome that you anticipate. But, more than just that, it may lead to mistrust and misjudgment of your substantive legal skills. Failure to present an idea effectively can be read to mean failure to understand a legal issue. It can lead the reader to become confused by your writing, frustrating them and ultimately causing them to bypass your guidance and analysis.

Consider the following examples of what can happen as a result of ineffective legal writing:

- On the issue of ineffective legal writing, one of the Supreme Court Justices has stated that, "[i]f someone uses improper grammar, you begin to think, well, maybe the person isn't as careful about his work, or his or her work, as he or she should be if he doesn't speak carefully."[6]
- "Poor writing by an attorney can result in any or all of the following: the court sanctioning the attorney; the client losing his or her legal claim; or the client becoming involved in unnecessary litigation."[7]

---

[6] Justice John Paul Stevens, *The Scribes Journal of Legal Writing*, 49 (2010).

[7] Wendy Davis, *Perspectives: Teaching Legal Research and Writing*, Consequences of Ineffective Writing, vol. 8, 1 (Winter 2000).

- Courts have indicated their displeasure with wordiness[8] and lack of clarity[9] in briefs and pleadings. Courts have dismissed complaints with grammatical errors,[10] and denied motions with misplaced punctuation marks.[11]
- For example, in *Laitram Corporation v. Cambridge Wire Cloth Company*,[12] the court ordered a $1000 fine to be paid by the lawyers for both parties, because the briefs lacked references to the record, relied on attorney argument as evidence, and cited inapplicable authority. The court stated that "counsel have in this case wasted this court's resources by playing in the rarified atmosphere of a debating society."[13]
- In *Julien v. Zeringue*,[14] the court imposed financial sanctions, equal to the defendant's attorney's fees, against the plaintiff's counsel. "Julien's counsel concedes that his unprofessional management over the preparation of this appeal resulted in 'burdening the appellate court with 'ragtag' and 'rough edge' performances with hurried work products.' We agree and sanction him personally under 28 U.S.C. § 1927 (1982)." *Julien v. Zeringue*, 864 F.2d 1572, 1575 (Fed. Cir. 1989). "The judicial process has been badly abused by Julien's counsel. For example, he continually missed deadlines, requested at least 10 extensions of time to file his briefs, and submitted a joint appendix 11 months after he was given extensive and explicit instructions on how to prepare and file a joint appendix. After being warned that no further time extensions would be granted, he missed the deadline for filing Julien's reply brief and joint appendix." *Id.* at 1575-1576.
- In a similar case, *Feliciano v. Rhode Island*,[15] the plaintiff's claim under the Americans with Disabilities Act was dismissed because the complaint was too vague. The court found that the complaint did not describe the claim in sufficient detail, nor did it allege facts to support the claim of denial of constitutional rights. The complaint also alleged that there were differences in interpretation in the two applicable federal laws, but did not articulate those differences, and therefore the court did not consider this allegation.
- In the case of *Hernandez v. N.Y. City Law Dept. Corp. Counsel*,[16] the court found that the lawyer's trial brief was extremely sloppy, intentionally misleading, and "dead wrong," and thus ordered the lawyer to show cause why he should not be sanctioned. The judge also ordered the lawyer to bring a supervisor to court "to discuss the overall poor quality of [the] brief in terms

---

8 *See Gordon v. Green*, 602 F.2d 743, 744–45 (5th Cir. 1979).

9 *See Slater v. Gallman*, 339 N.E.2d 863, 864 (N.Y. 1975).

10 *See, e.g., Duncan v. AT&T Communications*, 668 F. Supp. 232, 237 (S.D.N.Y. 1987).

11 *See, e.g., People v. Vasquez*, 520 N.Y.S.2d 99, 103 n.2 (N.Y. Crim. Ct. 1987).

12 919 F.2d 1579 (Fed. Cir. 1990).

13 *Id.* at 1584.

14 864 F.2d 1572 (Fed. Cir. 1989).

15 160 F.3d 780 (1st Cir. 1998).

16 1997 U.S. Dist. LEXIS 620 (S.D.N.Y. 1997).

of content, organization, and issues not included that should have been."

- In *Ky. B. Assn. v. Brow*,[17] a lawyer filed a one-and-a-half page brief that the court found to be "virtually incomprehensible." The court characterized it as "little more than fifteen unclear and ungrammatical sentences, slapped together as two pages of unedited text with an unintelligible message." The state bar charged the lawyer with incompetence, and he was suspended from the practice of law for sixty days and ordered to pay the costs of the bar action.

Given the amount of time and additional effort a non-native English speaker puts into preparing a legal document in English, having the guidance in that document ignored is an unacceptable outcome — yet, it happens all too frequently. Developing effective legal writing skills in English takes practice, but that practice can only follow from clear instructions on process, which this book provides.

[A] WHAT ARE THE RISKS OF INEFFECTIVE LEGAL WRITING?

The written word is everlasting. This can be a good thing if you are Shakespeare and you intend for your words to live on for generations. But, when you are writing documents that provide legal advice or even that assert your opinion on a matter, everlasting documents mean long-term potential liability.

Everything that you write, whether in the form of an email, memorandum, formal letter, or court document, creates a record of your words that can be used by others. Your harmless email to a colleague sharing your friendly advice on a case may ultimately be viewed by a document review attorney during a lawsuit related to that case, and your name will suddenly be in the spotlight if they decide that your email is pertinent to the case. The same could be said about subpoenas and other court orders directing you or the recipient of your messages to divulge all written communiqués.

Nothing that you write is safe from third-party review. Encrypted emails and hard drives have been breached by hackers and via court orders; shredded letters have been reconstructed; and locked files have been burglarized. In one instance, I recall a high-level official walking to work with a file in her hand that was taken when she was mugged, along with her purse and phone. It is unlikely the file was the target of the attack, but it is a clear reminder that written records can fall out of your control easily.

The point of all of this is that your words matter. Especially as a legal professional, your words carry a great deal of authority and are often interpreted and misinterpreted to suit the needs of the reader. Accordingly, it is essential that your words be carefully crafted, concisely written, and fully reviewed before they are released from your control. In the next section, we will consider how this goal manifests in American legal writing.

---

[17] 14 S.W.3d 916, 917 (Ky. 2000).

[B] WHAT MAKES AMERICAN LEGAL WRITING UNIQUE?

American legal writing is different from legal writing in many other parts of the world. For one thing, excessive litigation has led many lawyers to draft correspondence and contracts very conservatively, carefully avoiding any language that might lead to a lawsuit or an unwanted obligation. This, in turn, leads many American lawyers to draft short, concise statements rather than expansive explanations. Rather than making sure everything is included, we make sure only what is necessary is present.

This style of legal writing is new to many foreign legal practitioners and takes some getting used to. Here are some of the key elements of American legal writing that we will focus on in this book:

- Demand for Brevity
- Plain Legal English
- Clear Issue Identification
- Succinct Conclusions

[1] Demand for Brevity

> *When you wish to instruct, be brief; that men's minds take in quickly what you say, learn its lesson, and retain it faithfully. Every word that is unnecessary only pours over the side of a brimming mind.* — Cicero

The previous section explained how valuable your words are and how important it is that those words be carefully crafted. This also means that your writing should be as concise as possible without losing meaning. In some cultures, flowery language and extensive explanations are considered a sign of knowledge and experience in an area. The more ways you have to explain something, the more scholarly you are. This is not the case in American legal writing.

If you can think of ten ways to define a particular term, you have a decision to make — how is it being defined for use in this context. If there are several ways to describe an event, you must consider what would be the description most effective for your client. Rather than using superfluous or flowery language, American legal writing is generally succinct and often curt. Sentences are short and every word within those sentences was chosen intentionally, as the drafter recognizes the legal effect that each word creates.

Do not confuse brevity with over-simplification. Your goal should be to turn a five-page memorandum into a one-page email message without sacrificing meaning and without creating unwanted liability. But, if doing so requires you to ignore necessary explanations or exclude essential references, err on the side of inclusion rather than exclusion. Clear language is dependent not only upon concise statements, but also on complete information.

> "[Too] many lawyers approach a brief as if they are a waiter a cocktail party: 'Here are five arguments your honor. Take one.' That's wrong. A lawyer's job

is to tell the judge which one to take; that's what advocacy means. Any good advocate is selective. That doesn't mean you can't make your six arguments; it means that your best two better make up 90 percent of the brief."[18]

Writing concisely takes time and practice. It is much more difficult to write a concise letter than to write an extensive memorandum. As Blaise Pascal said, "I have made this [letter] longer, because I have not had the time to make it shorter."[19] Take the time to edit your drafts extensively and choose your words appropriately — your reader will appreciate the clarity, and you will appreciate the security in knowing that your intent is clear and your meaning unmistakable.

[2] Plain Legal English

Genius is the ability to reduce the complicated to the simple. — C.W. Ceram

The law is an exclusive domain in which to practice; but, our guidance as legal professionals should be capable of being understood by all. *Legalese* has penetrated the legal writing profession to such an extent that legal documents have been confined to a legal arena out of reach to non-lawyers. The law is meant to serve the public and should be accessible by all interested parties, regardless of knowledge of legalese. Writing in plain English is often one of the hardest skills for lawyers to develop, even though it should be a natural process.

"Plain English" is a concept that is meant to encourage simplified writing of technical concepts, including medicine, law, economics, and so forth. It is quite easy, especially for a professional in one of these fields, to choose words and methods of expression that hide true meaning from the reader and that ultimately protect the professional from criticism. This practice is archaic and weakens the ability of professionals to provide meaningful advice. In the law, there are still many cases in which legalese, the word used to define overcomplication of concepts through the use of uncommon legal words, are prominent.

Write so that you're understood. English is a hard language to learn, but it's an easy language to communicate in. There's no reason to put Latin in your brief. — Hon. Craig T. Enoch, Fifth Court of Appeals, Dallas, Texas

Writing in plain legal English means choosing words that convey the appropriate legal meaning but that do so without confusing the reader. This often means using shorter sentences or defining necessary legal terms. Here are a few tips to help you write in Plain Legal English:

- Keep sentences to a reasonable length (20 words on average);
- Use shorter words, where appropriate;

---

[18] Steven Stark, *Interview: Win Cases with Effective Writing, Be Concise; Avoid Adjectives and Archaic Terms*, Plain Language Association International, *available at* http://www.plainlanguagenetwork.org/legal/stark.html (accessed on September 29, 2012).

[19] *Provincial Letters: Letter XVI*, 1657. Original in French: "Je n'ai fait celle-ci plus longue que parce que je n'ai pas eu le loisir de la faire plus courte."

- Avoid double and triple negatives;
- Prefer the active voice;
- Keep related words together;
- Break up the text with headings;
- Avoid extensive cross-references;
- Avoid over-defining;
- Use recitals and purposes clauses.

[3] Clear Issue Identification

"The most important thing is to be accurate and intellectually honest in your arguments and state them clearly."[20] Furthermore, "[t]he law demands precision of its practitioners and penalizes those whose work is rush and sloppy."[21] For example, the Wisconsin Court of Appeals declared an appeal frivolous because the lawyer did not clearly identify the legal issue, lied about the facts, and tried to deceive the court regarding the client's actions and the court's prior rulings. As a result, the judge awarded the opposing party costs, fees, and reasonable attorney fees, and ordered the amount to be paid solely by the dishonest lawyer.[22]

In a similar example, the United States District Court for the Southern District of New York granted a motion to dismiss because the plaintiff's issues and complaint in general were so poorly drafted that it failed to state a claim for relief. The court further noted that "the court's responsibilities do not include cryptography, especially when the plaintiff is represented by counsel."[23]

Only through early and clear reflection will the lawyer be able to effectively ascertain the case's basic contentions and respective remedies. Lawyers who do not pinpoint the exact legal issues of their case, due to a lack time spent on understanding the facts or not thoroughly researching applicable laws, run the risk of obfuscating their claim and minimizing the chances of obtaining a favorable outcome.

Legal issues arise from reasonable disagreements on how legal precedent should be applied to a particular set of facts. Issues constitute the focal point of a legal controversy and are critical for a lawyer to identify in arguing the merits of the case. The first step in carving-out the legal issues is to understand the factual premise and context of the argument presented in your case. Once you have established this construct, it is imperative to organize your facts into an outline so as to prevent confusion over the sequence of events.

---

[20] Justice John Paul Stevens, *The Scribes Journal of Legal Writing*, 46 (2010).

[21] John C. Dernbach & Richard V. Singleton II, *A Practical Guide to Legal Writing and Legal Method*, 93 (Fred B. Rothman & Co. of Littleton Co., 1981).

[22] *Weiland v. Paulin*, 655 N.W.2d 204 (Wisc. Ct. App. 2002).

[23] *Duncan v. AT&T Communications*, 668 F. Supp. 232, 234 (S.D.N.Y. 1987).

The next task is to research and examine the relevant rules and case law that will comprise your framework for analysis. Lastly, you must apply the facts to your research to determine the outcome of the rules' application. By exercising your legal reasoning, you will then be able to state your conclusions with conviction and effectively litigate your cause of action.

[4] Succinct Conclusions

The conclusion of a legal document serves two purposes. First, it reminds the reader of the key issue and the logical outcome that follows from your analysis. Second, it reiterates what is being asked of the reader.

The conclusion of a legal document is not:

- An opportunity to raise arguments that did not conform to any of the section headings in the main text.
- A platform from which the writer can attack or criticize the other party or a particular precedent.
- A reiteration of the arguments already made in the main text.

Rather, the conclusion is your opportunity to "seal the deal" by highlighting the logic of the conclusion that you wish the reader to draw from your analysis. By this point in the document, the reader should already have a conclusion in mind. Thus, your role here is to solidify their assumption and validate their decision.

Your arguments should already have led the reader to your conclusion without explicitly stating it. Accordingly, when you state the conclusion, do so in concise, strong language. Some examples of strong conclusions follow below.

The second crucial element to a conclusion in a legal document is the recommended course of action. This will differ depending on the type of document you are drafting.

- Internal Legal Memoranda: A legal memo that you plan to submit to a senior associate or partner at a law firm, for instance, should recommend a course of action to take based upon the analysis of precedent in the document. The language should be clear and unequivocal. The reader should know exactly what action is being recommended.
- Correspondence to a Client or Colleague: The legal letter may be recommending a particular action for the client or colleague to take, or it may be informative only. If action is being recommended, provide enough detail to avoid the need for the reader to contact you for clarification. Whether or not action is being requested, be sure to include proper contact information so that the reader can reach out to you if necessary.
- Court Briefs: there is no room for error in a court brief. You will likely have a limit on the number of words you can include, making it even more important to provide a succinct analysis and concise conclusion. In this type of document, your conclusion will include a prayer for relief — that is, a brief reiteration of what you would like the court to do (e.g., grant the motion to dismiss).

To many writers, the conclusion is an afterthought. Bear in mind that this is the last piece of information that a reader will have in mind when they put down your letter, brief, or memorandum. It will stand out in their minds and may be the only part of the document that the reader paid much attention to (unfortunately). This makes it essential that your conclusion is powerful and concise enough to form an accurate picture of the essence of your document.

[C] LEGAL DOCUMENTS: AN OVERVIEW

In this book, and in your practice, you will encounter several types of legal documents. Our focus will be on the most common types — case briefs, legal memoranda, and legal correspondence. However, there are many unique legal documents in the United States. Below is a partial list of those documents with brief explanations for each one:

- Case Brief: A case brief is a concise summary of the key elements of a single case. It is used by attorneys both as an exercise in extracting the key legal substance from a case and also as a quick reference to that case, should it be needed later. The case brief is neutral in tone, and, aside from any recommendations added by the author, is not meant to persuade or predict. It is not generally distributed outside the office. A sample case brief is found in Appendix B.

- Legal Memorandum: A legal memorandum, also known as an office memorandum, is a comprehensive analysis of a legal issue, often a question arising from a client's case. The legal memorandum is usually prepared by junior attorneys through extensive case law and statutory research, and is presented to the attorney managing the case. The legal memorandum is predictive in nature and is not intended to persuade the reader. The memo may be used to inform the legal brief submitted to the court, but it is not generally distributed outside the office. A sample legal memorandum is found in Appendix B.

- Demand Letter: A demand letter is a document drafted and sent by an attorney to another party with the intent to persuade them to take a certain action. A sample demand letter is found in Appendix B.

- Opinion Letter: An opinion letter is a document drafted and sent by an attorney to a client with the intent to answer a specific inquiry and provide legal advice. A sample opinion letter is found in Appendix B.

- Contracts: A contract is a legally binding agreement entered into by two or more parties who create performance obligations for one another. Contracts are discussed in chapter 6.

- Pleadings: The pleadings are the formal documents initiating a case. In general, they include the complaint (filed by the plaintiff), the answer (filed by the defendant), and any counterclaims (filed by the defendant). Each state has unique terms for what it considers to be "pleadings."

- Appellate Briefs: The appellate brief is filed with an appellate court in order to initiate a review of the decision of the trial court for error. The brief must clearly state the alleged error of the trial court and must also state the standard of review (i.e., the amount of deference the appellate court must give to the trial court).

- Summons: The summons is a document issued to a defendant informing them that they are being sued and providing them with details about the suit such as when they must appear in court and if they must respond to the summons. It is one form of process that may be served upon a defendant to initiate a lawsuit.

- Certificate of Service: The last page of a pleading generally includes a certificate of service. This short statement confirms to the court that the plaintiff has properly served process upon the defendant.

- Process: This is the broad term used to refer to the legal document issued to a defendant in a civil or criminal trial to inform them of the nature of the lawsuit against them. Process may include a summons, subpoena, warrant, or other document. Service of process is required in most jurisdictions for the court to obtain jurisdiction over the defendant.

Chapter 3

MAKING YOUR WRITING EFFECTIVE

[A] INTRODUCTION

This section of the text will focus on general effective writing skills. It is wise to start with some techniques and styles that apply to all legal writing. Given that this book is primarily for foreign law students and practitioners, we will focus on areas in which non-native speakers tend to make mistakes.

Topics Covered in This Chapter:

- Word Choice
- Sentence Structure
- Paragraph Structure and Transitions
- Gender and Number
- Common Misspellings and Definitional Errors
- Transitions and Punctuation
- Quotations and Paraphrasing

[B] WORD CHOICE

The measure of a drafter's success lies in the utility of the written document to the client.[24]

Complexity in legal drafting is often caused by poor word choice and sentence structure, not by the complexity of the subject matter. Word choice refers to the process of selecting the most accurate and descriptive terms to describe a concept or action, while maintaining meaning and simplicity. In other words, your writing should be clear and direct.

To write effectively, ambiguous words should be avoided. For instance, when you read the expression "and/or," what meaning do you attach to those words? Is it required or optional? The result is confusion, and likely misinterpretation by the reader, which could lead to liability for the drafter and his or her client. Effective drafting requires the drafter to think more carefully about the relationship between

[24] Lenne Eidson Espenscheid, *Contract Drafting: Powerful Prose in Transactional Practice*, 110 (ABA 2010).

the words and to decide affirmatively which meaning should be attached to those words.

One area in which ambiguity rears its ugly head is in the use of superfluous or unnecessary words. Lawyers in the United States and many countries around the world are taught to learn the language of law. To some professors, and thus to their students, this can mean adopting a more complex and convoluted vocabulary designed to emphasize a lawyer's command of the language and to in some cases to intimidate non-lawyers into taking certain actions.

Legalese, as it has come to be known in the United States, weakens a legal argument by concealing the issue, leading the reader astray through uncomfortable grammar choices, and ultimately distracting the reader from the point of the document. It has begun to fade away from legal correspondence and to some extent from legal briefs. Yet, legalese is alive and well in contracts. An online series in *Bloomberg Businessweek Magazine* summed up the effect of legalese in contracts: "The phenomenon [of legalese] causes most businesspeople, and even many other lawyers, to give up before ever trying to understand what the contract says."[25] This approach to legal writing is not only less effective than clear, concise, and plain English writing; it is also damaging to the writer's reputation as a legal professional.

Lawyers, both inexperienced and accomplished, often fall into the trap of using language that may sound sophisticated, but is unnecessary and confusing. To avoid this downfall of our profession, you must be precise and clear and learn to use more precise language to express your point. It should not be challenging for your audience to decipher the intent of your legal correspondence.

As opposed to the flowery, verbose language of legalese, plain English demonstrates your analytical skills through concise communication to inform your audience of the issues presented in your case and the proposed solution. Formality should be avoided, and legal terms should only be used to explain a technical term or point.

The problem with eliminating legalese from our language diet is that many of us have grown accustomed to it and have relied upon it as a crutch in our legal documents. Rather than concentrating on effective legal research and developing strong legal arguments, we insert nonsensical words and expressions that we hope will lead a non-lawyer to develop either trust (clients) or fear (opposing parties) in us. In too many cases, these efforts backfire and lead us to scramble to explain what we meant with our words.

A better option is to spend time on effective legal research and also on simplifying our language. To reduce our reliance on legalese, we can begin by opting for simpler word choices that convey the same meaning as legal terminology we might have preferred. Below is a list of superfluous expressions that are unnecessary in effective legal writing, along with a suggested alternative that conveys the same meaning:

---

[25] Nick Leiber, *Demystifying Legalese in Contracts, Part I*, Bloomberg Businessweek (2009), *available at* http://www.businessweek.com/smallbiz/running_small_business/archives/2009/08/demystifying_le.html (accessed September 29, 2012).

Legalese Expression:	Plain English Substitute:
A large number of	Many
Along the lines of	Like
At the time at which	When
By means of	By
Pursuant to the provisions of	Under
At this point in time	Now
Notwithstanding the fact that	Even though, although
Prior to	Before
Subsequent to	After
Until such time as	Until
By reason of the fact that	Because
Give rise to	Cause
Due to the fact that	Because
With the result that	So that

Making simpler word choices that convey the same meaning will not only help you to shorten your document substantially, it will also ensure that your meaning is not lost within a jumble of legal jargon. Maintaining your meaning is a critical component of providing effective legal advice. Proper word choice is the first step in achieving that goal.

[C] SUPERFLUOUS LANGUAGE

> *Omit needless words. This requires not that the writer make all his sentences short, or that he avoid all detail and treat his subjects only in outline, but that every word tell.* —W. Strunk, Jr., & E. White, *The Elements of Style* 17 (3d ed. 1979).

Lawyers are busy people. We face tight deadlines for nearly everything we do, forcing us in some cases to draft hasty letters and emails, or in some cases, even briefs and memoranda. In our rush, we may leave out essential details, fail to quote a crucial case or statute, or disclose information we did not intend to disclose. The consequences of such hasty writing are obvious.

What is less obvious is the equally detrimental impact of overly wordy legal documents. We may inadvertently assume that a lengthy document is more legally sound than a short document and that our longer explanations indicate that we spent a great deal of time on a document. In fact, the opposite is true.

There is a purpose to every word in every document that you write, and any superfluous discussion will only obfuscate and weaken your main contentions. As attorneys, our profession is to effectively argue each point. The more efficiently you can accomplish this task, the faster the end result, meaning less cost to the client, less time taken from the judge, and more opportunity to take on new cases. To avoid using superfluous language in your legal correspondence, you must ensure that each word contributes to the overall objective and structure of your writing.

Unnecessarily wordy documents are often less effective than concise documents. Extra words may confuse the issue, or the reader; distract the reader from the central issue or request; and may disclose information that need not be disclosed. The good news is that it is not overly time-consuming to write effective, concise legal documents. The key is to eliminate superfluous language.

In order to ensure clear and concise language in your legal documents, keep the following pointers in mind:

- Only include words that have good reason to exist in the document.
- Separate lengthy sentences into two or more short sentences.
- Keep each sentence to about 20 words.
- Avoid strings of words (e.g., sell, give, bequeath, assign . . . TRANSFER) that mean the same thing.
- Write in the active voice whenever possible.
- Avoid double negatives (e.g., "Buyer shall never fail to inspect the goods"; "Buyer shall inspect the goods.").
- Present a clear topic sentence first and use only supporting sentences that actually connect directly to that topic sentence.

With all of your legal documents, conduct a review to ensure that you have eliminated superfluous language. Your resulting documents will be shorter, more powerful, and will ultimately be more effective. To practice this skill, complete the exercise below.

EXERCISE: SUPERFLUOUS LANGUAGE

Revise these sentences to eliminate the unnecessary words:

1. In a similar case, the court in the case of *United States v. Smith*, ruled that Smith, the employee, was able to deduct from his gross income any monies that he had embezzled and then promptly reimbursed to his employer, during the twelve months that the monies were taken, but Smith was not permitted to deduct the stolen monies that he had repaid in the following twelve months.

2. Please be advised that I am in receipt of your letter dated July 25, 2012 from your office located in Boston, Massachusetts, in regards to the above matter, *Spann v. Johnson*, and please be informed that I have enclosed below my response and demands in this matter, which have been sent via certified U.S. mail. Please note that I await your response at your earliest convenience.

3. In submitting this motion for summary judgment before the court, I, as defense counsel, on behalf of my client, hereby interpret the statute and common law to support my client's case that he did not commit the required elements of assault with a deadly weapon and thereby this case should be dismissed for a lack of evidence on the merits.

4. Seller hereby agrees to sell, convey, transfer, assign and relinquish all possession of 1000 stocks to buyer to be sold at.50 cents a share.

5. Whereas, in consideration of the mutually agreed upon covenants of party A and party B, this contractual agreement is hereby duly executed and all provisions will be faithfully performed upon the date contracted to by the respective parties.

Suggested solutions can be found in Appendix A.

[D] SENTENCE STRUCTURE

> *To get the right word in the right place is a rare achievement. To condense the diffused light of a page of thought into the luminous flash of a single sentence, is worthy to rank as a prize composition just by itself . . . . Anybody can have ideas — the difficulty is to express them without squandering a quire of paper on an idea that ought to be reduced to one glittering paragraph.* — Mark Twain

Once you have selected the right words to use, stringing them together into an effective sentence should be an easier task. Sentence structure is a critical element in maintaining meaning as well. Placing the right words in the wrong places in your sentence can change the meaning of the sentence and lead to misinterpretation.

The subject of the sentence naturally longs to be near the verb. Separating the two in a sentence can lead to confusion and possible incorrect association of a subject with the wrong verb. How might you change the following examples to make sure that the subject is connected to the verb effectively?

- Example: Sarah, clearly startled by the flashing police lights, crashed her car.
- Example: The assertion that schoolchildren should be given equal opportunities to succeed in their attainment of education and that they should not be discriminated against on the basis of race is well founded in case law.

We might consider revising these examples as follows:

- Clearly startled by the flashing police lights, Sarah crashed her car.
    - *Sarah, clearly startled by the flashing police lights, crashed her car.*
- Case law supports the assertion that schoolchildren should be given equal opportunities to succeed in their attainment of education and that they should not be discriminated against on the basis of race.
    - *The assertion that schoolchildren should be given equal opportunities to succeed in their attainment of education and that they should not be discriminated against on the basis of race is well founded in case law.*

[E] CLEAR SENTENCES

In addition to removing superfluous language, good legal writers tend to prefer short, direct sentences that carry a strong impact. Using unnecessary words hides the impact and meaning of the sentence. Consider the following example:

- Original sentence:

  "We have taken under advisement the matter of Mr. Brown's assertion that the firm improperly billed him for work on his merger case."

- Improved sentence:

  "We are considering whether the firm improperly billed Mr. Brown for work on his merger case."

- Most effective sentence:

  "We are considering whether Mr. Brown was improperly billed by the firm."

[F] TRANSITIONS

A transition is a connecting word or phrase that links one paragraph to the next. Keeping ideas together is essential for maintaining the flow of the document and also for indicating to a reader how different ideas should be related to one another.

Transitions should be seen as the glue that holds the paragraphs in a document together. Without them, the paragraphs would float like independent islands in a sea of confusion for your reader. Effectively using transitions between paragraphs gives the reader a complete picture of the message you are trying to convey, no matter how complex it may be.

Here are a few tips for effective transitions:

- If you cannot identify an appropriate transition between two thoughts, you are likely missing an essential element in the discussion that needs to be explained before moving on.
- Vary your transitions throughout the document to avoid redundancy and select language that most appropriately connects the specific thoughts together.
- Repetitive transitions, which repeat a few key words from the previous paragraph, can be highly effective, especially when connecting complex ideas.

Below are a few examples of effective transitions:

1. The law firm of Jones and Smith has enjoyed a marked increase in its domestic client base. New developments in the intellectual property sector have facilitated this increase in growth. All of this has helped the firm increase its profits by 35% this year.

   These impressive profits are also reflective of the firm's increasing international presence. Last year, for example, it opened offices in Dubai and Shanghai.

2. The firm's newest client, John Jones, faces serious substantial fines and potential incarceration for his alleged acts. He has been charged with assault, larceny and trespass.

   Each of these charges carries a minimum fine of $1,000 and 30 days in prison.

[G] SENTENCE SEQUENCING AND PARAGRAPH STRUCTURE

The order of text in a paragraph (or sentence) can often have a substantial impact on the meaning and comprehension of the text. The main idea of the paragraph should be presented as clearly and as early in the paragraph as possible. That idea should then resonate throughout the rest of the paragraph as supporting sentences strengthen the initial message and leave the reader with a sense that the idea has been substantiated.

Each paragraph should contain a thesis sentence and between one and four supporting sentences. Each supporting sentence should have a clear and logical relationship to the thesis sentence. The last sentence in the paragraph should be emphatic and should emphasize the veracity of the thesis sentence.

- Example of a poorly drafted paragraph:
  - There are a lot of cases that discuss child pornography and how tech-savvy pedophiles abuse the law. One such case, the Jacobs case, is controversial because courts are in disagreement over how its holding should be applied to similar situations. Because of this, it is clear that the law in this area needs to be updated.
- Properly written, this paragraph might read:
  - The law prohibiting child pornography is outdated. It has been abused by tech-savvy pedophiles on numerous occasions, such as in the *Jones* case, the *Smith* case and also in the much debated *Jacobs* case.

Below are some pointers for effective paragraphing:

- A thesis sentence should begin (or end) the paragraph.
- Each supporting sentence should be related to the thesis sentence.
- The paragraph should contain at least two sentences and each sentence should be short.
- Tense, number, and person should not change throughout the paragraph.

[H] AMBIGUOUS DRAFTING AND WORD CHOICE

Eliminating superfluous language, effectively connecting sentences together in a paragraph, and transitioning between paragraphs in a document will go a long way in ensuring that the message is conveyed to the reader. However, there are other pitfalls that we face in legal drafting.

One of these pitfalls is improper or ambiguous word choice. Inserting a word that is open to interpretation or that can be confused by the reader lights the pathway to a dispute in the future. Word choice plays a significant role not only in contract drafting, but also in other legal documents, such as demand letters and legal memoranda.

To avoid ambiguity, skilled legal writers should keep the following in mind:

- Reduce the use of "shall" to create an obligation; prefer the use of "must" to create an obligation.
- Avoid the use of "and/or" and instead decide which of those words you should use.
- Always capitalize defined or proper terms.
- Be particularly attentive to word choice when drafting numbers, dates, and denominations of currency.
- Avoid acronyms and abbreviations unless they are widely utilized.

Legal documents should not leave anything open to interpretation. There may be instances in which ambiguity appears to be beneficial to your client to keep an option open; however, a skilled lawyer can easily find a way to use that ambiguity against your client, leading to more litigation than necessary.

Practice your skill at identifying ambiguity and making proper word choices with the following exercise.

EXERCISE: DRAFTING TO AVOID AMBIGUITY

Review the following sentences and determine whether they are drafted clearly and effectively. If not, redraft them as clearly as possible.

1. These out-of-pocket expenses include investigation, witness preparation, travel costs, and a $.10 per sheet fee for photocopying.

2. I bequeath my property, The White House, located at 1600 Pennsylvania Avenue, N.W. Washington, D.C. 20500 to my son, Alfred, when he turns twenty-one years old or comes of age.

3. I will sell you my land at 800 55th Street, New York, New York for $500,000.

4. The homeowners association does not allow for any property owner to plant any variety of tall trees and must remove any tree planted before 1950 at their own expense.

5. Lessee may select to arbitrate and/or litigate in the United States and/or Germany.

6. The deed for a parcel of land was in the name of both husband and wife. The husband took out a mortgage with Bank to pay for the property. The husband died. Bank contends the wife is still obligated to pay the loan, while the wife contends she is not.

7. A disability insurance policy states that it covers disability for 52 weeks from the effective date of the policy. Later in the policy's language, it indicates that the insurance company will not be liable for disabilities that arise within the first 15 days of the policy period.

8. Nation A agreed with Nation B that all land east of the Blue River would belong to Nation A. Since signing the border agreement, there have been three seasons of unprecedented rainfall, and the Blue River has grown from one mile across to three miles across.

9. The United States has agreed to buy Grade A beef from Canada at a price of $.70 per pound.

10. To be considered for appointment as a government official, you must have obtained a four year college diploma or its educational equivalent or; full time military service with current active duty or an honorable discharge.

Suggested solutions can be found in Appendix A.

[I] PARALLEL STRUCTURE

Parallel structure refers to the pattern of words in a sentence and helps to give equal importance to each of the ideas in that sentence. The best way to connect ideas in a sentence to ensure that they are in parallel form is to use a coordinating conjunction such as "and" or "or." Consider the following examples:

Example 1:

- The senior partner at the firm is responsible for identifying new clients, representing the firm at meetings, and also makes decisions on firm resources. [Not parallel structure].
- The senior partner at the firm is responsible for identifying new clients, representing the firm at meetings, and making decisions on firm resources. [Parallel structure].

Example 2:

- Lawyers tend to function efficiently, coherently, and in an organized manner. [Not parallel structure].
- Lawyers tend to function efficiently, coherently, and carefully. [Parallel structure].

EXERCISE — PARALLEL STRUCTURE

Review each of the following examples and determine whether the sentence structure is effective or whether it is likely to confuse the reader. If it is confusing, redraft the sentences to be more clear and effective.

1. Each Member hereby agrees to execute such other and further statements of interest and holdings, designations, powers of attorney and other instruments necessary to comply with any applicable laws, rules, or regulations. The Members each

agree to cooperate, and to execute and deliver in a timely fashion any and all additional documents necessary to effectuate the purposes of the Company and this Operating Agreement.

2. The 2012 version of the D.C. Superior Court Code includes ten additional offenses, remedial measures for victims of violent crime, and creates a new enhanced penalty section that was redrafted to comply with the 2012 Judicial Sentencing Guidelines.

3. The seller must be reasonable and act in good faith when conducting business under the Uniform Commercial Code. Such general terminology provides the seller and the buyer neither with an understanding of potential causes of action or mechanisms for recovery.

Suggested solutions can be found in Appendix A.

[J] VOICE

Most of us learned in grammar school that writing in the active voice is the preferred method of communication. This means that the subject in the sentence takes the action, rather than the subject being the recipient of the action. Consider the following examples:

Example 1:

- After reviewing the recording, it was concluded that the suspect had lied to the investigator. [Passive voice].
- After reviewing the recording, the jury concluded that the suspect had lied to the investigator. [Active voice].

Example 2:

- Even though the judge summarily dismissed the complaint, arguments against dismissal continued to be made.
- Even though the judge summarily dismissed the complaint, the losing party continued to make arguments against dismissal.

Passive voice is useful when we wish to hide the identity of the actor or when we wish to emphasize the action over the actor. However, in most cases, a skilled legal writer will write in the active voice.

To further enhance your ability to identify and eliminate passive voice from your legal writing, practice with the following exercise.

EXERCISE: ACTIVE/ PASSIVE VOICE

Convert each of the following passive sentences into active voice, if you believe it is necessary to make the sentence most effective.

1. The fee-simple interest will be conveyed by them to the defendant.

2. It was demonstrated by the plaintiff that the defendant was paid for his interest in the promissory note.

3. The lawyer was sanctioned by the judge for misappropriating client funds.

4. By signing this contract, all conditions are agreed to by buyer.

5. The parcels will be delivered after payment by the seller.

6. The items will be accepted by the buyer in their current condition.

7. The embassy will have been constructed by the contractor by November.

8. The parcel will be rented by the lessor for a reasonable price.

9. The coast guard discovered that the cargo had been stolen from the ship. (To emphasize the action of the sentence).

10. The term length is not to be exceeded for any reason by any party.

Suggested solutions can be found in Appendix A.

[K] REVIEW: LEGAL STYLE

Effective legal writing is not rocket science; however, it takes practice and repetition. The skills that we discussed in this section may have been reminders of earlier lessons that we have forgotten, or they may be elements of writing that we never fully understood. But, each of these skills contributes to the development of high-impact legal documents that are more likely to result in your desired outcome than hastily prepared and poorly drafted documents.

To help you establish a routine of properly applying grammar and style rules, consider developing a checklist of issues that you tend to overlook, such as converting passive to active voice, maintaining parallel structure, or excluding superfluous language. Post that list near your computer or wherever you prepare your legal documents and refer to it each time you write. Within a short period of time, you will have adopted the routine of checking for these issues and can count yourself among the group of skilled legal writers. To get you started, I have prepared the following list of common errors:

Effective Legal Writing Checklist

- Words
  - Have you replaced legalese with plain English language?
  - Have you eliminated the use of "shall" and "and/or"?
  - Have you eliminated ambiguous terms?
- Sentences
  - Are your sentences concise (approx. 20 words)?
  - Can anything be removed without losing meaning?

    - Are your sentences drafted in the active voice?
- Paragraphs
    - Did you start or end with a clear topic sentence?
    - Are all supporting sentences related to the topic sentence?
    - Did you use more than one but less than four sentences?
- Entire Document
    - Have you effectively applied transitions between paragraphs?
    - Did you thoroughly review for spelling and punctuation mistakes?
    - Have you utilized section headings to divide groups of ideas?

[L] A FEW FINAL POINTERS

[1] Punctuation

Semicolons and commas: Use semicolons and commas in their appropriate place. Commas separate independent clauses connected by a coordinating conjunction, establish pauses, and divide lists (serial commas). Semicolons connect two independent clauses not connected by a coordinating conjunction.

- Example: A case brief should include a section on facts, issues, analysis, and a conclusion.
- Example: A poorly drafted appellate brief reflects negatively on the lawyer; it could even lead to open criticism by the judge.

Hyphens and dashes: A hyphen is used to connect phrasal adjectives to nouns and pronouns.

- Example: This is the final-cut of the film.

An em-dash is used to emphasize independent but connected points to a sentence.

- Example: I took pains to explain to the student that dumping — referring to international trade — had nothing to do with trash removal.
- Tip: In MS Word, the em-dash can be inserted from the Insert\Symbols menu.

[2] Spacing

- Correspondence and legal memoranda should include indented paragraphs (usually 0.5 inch before the first line).
- Contracts should use hanging indents so that text lines up on top of itself rather than under the bullet or number of the line.
    - Example: Buyer shall have 30 days from the date of delivery to remit full payment to Seller at the address provided in section 4.1.

- If documents are single spaced, insert one blank line between paragraphs. If they are double spaced, this is not necessary.
- Always write with left alignment — it is easier on the reader's eyes.

[3] Capitalization

- Do not overcapitalize. Capitalization should be reserved for proper names, names of statutes, and names of specific courts that you are referring to (or the U.S. Supreme Court in all cases).
    - Example: The Second Circuit Court of Appeals upheld the lower court's verdict.
    - Example: Once the Affordable Care Act takes effect, the number of uninsured citizens will likely diminish.
- Capitalization of terms in a contract can indicate that the term is a defined term. If the term is not in fact in the defined terms section, it may be misinterpreted by the other party.

[4] Acronyms

- Acronyms are very common in usage in the United States, but they can lead to confusion when the same acronym refers to different things.
    - Example: DHS may mean the U.S. Department of Homeland Security or the Michigan Department of Human Services.
- The first time you use an acronym, write-out the full name and include the abbreviated version in parentheses afterward.
    - Example: Federal agents from the Department of Homeland Security (DHS) discovered a stash of stolen money in the gang leader's garage.
- You can find numerous online lists of acronyms common in the legal industry. One such list is published by the University of Washington School of Law Library, available at http://lib.law.washington.edu/pubs/acron.html.

Chapter 4

DRAFTING CORRESPONDENCE

[A] INTRODUCTION

This chapter will address the most common form of legal writing — correspondence. Whether drafting a simple email to an associate at a firm in the United States, or summarizing a key strategy meeting for a senior partner or important client, correspondence can serve as one of the most valuable mechanisms to communicate your message effectively. We will focus on developing clear and concise writing with strong action statements to significantly enhance your emails, faxes and letters.

Topics Covered in This Chapter:

- Knowing your Audience
- Greetings and Salutations
- Brevity
- The Risks and Rewards of Electronic Documents
- Closings and Follow-ups
- Attachments and Related Material
- Technology Tips
- Sample Documents

[B] GENERAL CORRESPONDENCE

Outside of the United States, a great deal of correspondence continues to be drafted on formal letterhead and delivered by courier or post to the intended recipient. Secure email formats and servers have given confidence to many U.S. legal professionals in their reliance on email as the preferred method of communication.

Email has obvious benefits, such as instant delivery, return receipt and delivery confirmation built-in, attachments rather than enclosures, and economically speaking, email is a low-cost communication solution. However, it has risks as well, which we will address in this chapter. Printed letters sent by courier or post tend to be viewed as more formal, and demand more attention than an email. However, when working across borders, quickly and affordably sending correspondence by post can be exceedingly difficult.

Let's begin with some helpful hints for ensuring that printed correspondence, whether it is sent by post, courier, or scanned in as an email attachment, should include all of the following elements:

- ► Always on letterhead;
- ► Proper form of greeting;
  - ► E.g., "Dear Mr. Jones; Dear Senator Schumer";
- ► Open with the reason for writing;
- ► Provide adequate analysis; yet be brief;
  - ► Most letters should be less than one page long;
- ► Use appropriate closing with follow-up details;
  - ► E.g., "Please do not hesitate to contact me at (202) 555-1212 should you have any additional questions concerning this matter."

[C] CLIENT ADVICE LETTER

When you draft a letter to a client, you should keep in mind the following:

1. What questions should this document answer?
2. Who is my reader?
3. What is my reader's relationship to me?
4. How much does my reader know about the subject and answer?
5. What is my reader's attitude about the subject?
6. What does my reader need to know to understand the answer?
7. Why am I writing this?
8. What constraints do I have?

Teresa Goodwin Phelps, *Writing Strategies for Practicing Attorneys*, 23 GONZAGA L.R. 155, 164 (1987).

Based on your responses to these questions, the format of your letter should meet the needs of the inquiry. Here is a sample layout you might use when providing a client with advice:

1. Opening Paragraph:
   a. Customized pleasantries and introductions, (i.e., thank you for coming into the office)
   b. Define legal question and answer it
2. Fact Summary:
   a. Verify accuracy, protect your analysis

3. Legal Analysis:
    a. Summary of the law and your legal conclusions, not full recitation of memorandum
    b. Full citations are generally not necessary, (reference statute, cases)
    c. Cater language to the sophistication of our client
4. Advice:
    a. Explain solutions and pros and cons for each
    b. Do not make guarantees
5. Closing paragraph:
    a. What will happen next? (come into the office, writing a letter, mediation)
    b. Make yourself available
    c. Pleasantries

Client Advice Letter Formalities to Remember:

1. On letterhead;
2. Date;
3. Client name and address;
4. File reference;
5. Greeting, and salutation;
6. Additional suggestions: "Attny-Client Privl/Attny-Work Priv" designation;
7. Tone is critical to effective client-oriented legal writing; Anticipate client's reaction.

EXERCISE: EDIT AND REWRITE THE FOLLOWING DEMAND LETTER

[Date]

Mr. Adam Smith
General Counsel
Drill Baby Drill, LLC
500 5th Avenue, Suite B
New York, NY 10036

Dear Mr. Smith,

It has come to our attention that you recently assigned a drilling contract that had been awarded to your company by the Colombian Department of Mines and Energy, to a Chinese firm. This is a violation of the non-assignment clause found in section

10.8 of our agreement, dated on June 14, 2010. Additionally, this may violate Colombian law and create liability for the Department of Mines and Energy.

As you know, your firm entered into an exclusive drilling contract with the Colombian Department of Mines and Energy on June 14, 2010. In that agreement, you were provided with the right to drill for oil and gas in the Soledad region of Colombia for a period not to exceed twelve months. The Colombian government would receive 10% of all net profits earned from the sale of any extracted commodities.

It has come to our attention that rather than arranging to drill in Soledad with your own labor and equipment, approximately one month after having signed the contract, you assigned your rights under this contract to a Chinese drilling company, which has since begun to drill off the coast of Soledad. As you are aware, the Colombian government already has contracts in place with public and private Chinese entities that provide licenses to drill in specific regions of the country. However, procurement regulations under Colombian law prohibit drilling licenses from being issued to any one country for more than five percent of Colombian territory. Combined with existing Chinese drilling contracts, your assignment provides drilling access to Chinese companies for over 5.4% of Colombian territory.

As a result of your actions, we are requesting a meeting with you in Bogotá, Colombia to discuss potential resolutions to this matter. Please note the urgency of this matter and make every effort to schedule a meeting with us promptly by contacting my office. Should the matter be left unresolved ten days from the date of this letter, we will have no choice but to take action against you. Thank you for your prompt attention to this matter.

Sincerely,

Juan Sanchez, Esq.
General Counsel
Colombian Department of Mines and Energy

Sample answer can be found in Appendix B.

[D] EMAIL COMMUNICATIONS

Email has certainly become the preferred method of corresponding in the United States and in many other parts of the world. It is fast, cheap, and relatively easy to prepare and send. Yet all of these benefits point to the result that email is often used in a haphazard and unprofessional manner. The way that email is used today is far removed from the way the formal letter was used in the past.

When you communicate with your colleagues in the United States at law firms or other entities, you likely already do so via email. This not only allows you to efficiently communicate and send legal guidance back and forth, it also provides you with a record of the transmission and the ability to copy a number of parties, even without the recipient being aware. In addition, modern technology allows users to send electronic communications via secure channels to ensure that the information in the message does not fall into the wrong hands.

There are a number of risks that you run when you become accustomed to communicating professional matters via email. For starters:

- You risk clicking send too quickly and omitting attachments, additional recipients, or editing the text.
- You risk inadvertently sending the email to the wrong recipient due to the use of auto-complete in the address field.
- You risk transmission errors, such as ending up in the junk folder of the intended recipient.
- You risk having your message lost in a sea of incoming messages to the intended recipient.

All of these risks can be avoided with a few simple steps. It is crucial to adopt these as routines in your email so as to develop a reputation for being a careful and thoughtful drafter.

- ► Email tips:
  - ► Insert recipient address *after* drafting and reviewing the email.
  - ► If attaching documents, attach them *before* drafting the message.
  - ► Ensure that auto spell-check is on.
  - ► Review the message carefully before sending.
  - ► Ensure that a signature line with contact information is always included.
  - ► When editing text in an email response, use track changes.

EXERCISE: EMAIL CORRESPONDENCE

Edit and redraft the following email following the tips discussed above:

Greetings, Mr. Smith

I hope this email finds you well. I write to you on behalf of my client, the Colombian Department of Mines and Energy. Why did you not respond to my last correspondence? As a reminder, I wrote to you and said the Department of Mines and Energy would be pursuing damages and would terminate our contract with you should you not respond within ten days of the dated letter.

A claim has been filed by the Department of Mines and Energy and should have been received by your offices. We will not be ignoring this matter and expect a response promptly.

Sincerely,

Juan Sanchez, Esq.

Sample answer can be found in Appendix B.

[E] TECHNOLOGY TIPS

The following tips apply to Microsoft Outlook 2008 and 2010 (2011 for Apple users).

[1] Delaying Message Delivery

There are two principal reasons you may want to delay the delivery of your email message. First, you may want to avoid the problems that you read about above, which typically result from drafting a message and clicking send before you have had an opportunity to digest your response. In my experience, I have found many attorneys who routinely send a message and then later review the message in their "Sent Items" folder to make sure they said everything that they intended to. Rather than go through this useless exercise, you can use the "Delay Delivery" function.

A second reason to favor this tool is to give yourself an opportunity to draft your messages when it is convenient for you, and then have them delivered at a time when they will be most effective. For instance, you may want your message to appear in the recipient's inbox at precisely 8:00 am, when you know the recipient arrives at the office and begins reviewing messages. Alternatively, you may want a message to be sent on a future date to comply with a particular deadline, such as the last day to cancel a particular service that you have been using.

To utilize this feature, follow the steps below.

STEP 1: Begin a new email message in MS Outlook.

STEP 2: Select the tab or ribbon labeled "Options." Then select the "Delay Delivery" button to get the screen shown below.

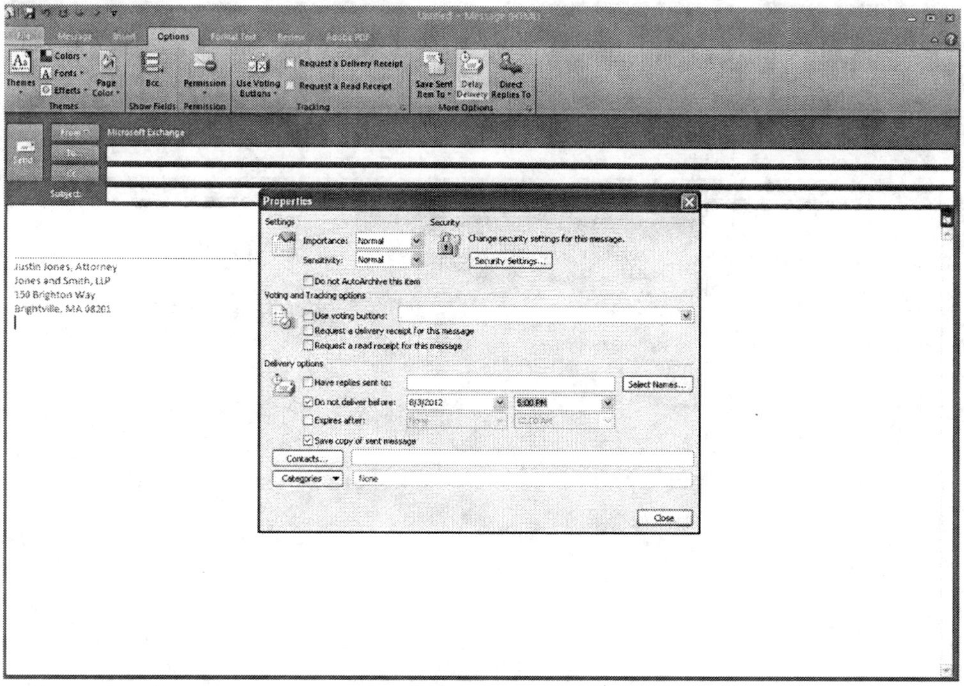

STEP 3: Under the section for "Delivery Options," make sure the box is checked for "Do not deliver before." Enter the date and time when you would like the message sent from your outbox. Click close. Next, send the message as you would normally. It will wait in your outbox until the date and time that you selected.

IMPORTANT NOTE: Your computer must be online and Outlook must be open at the intended date and time of delivery or else it will not send.

[2] Requesting Return Receipt or Read Notification

In the United States legal community, return receipts and read receipts are less common than they used to be. The reason for this change in culture in part is that email systems have become much more reliable, almost guaranteeing that if your message was properly addressed and sent, it did in fact arrive in the recipients inbox (or junk mail folder). However, it is a common convention used by non-U.S. lawyers and may be used when transmitting time-sensitive documents as well.

To utilize the "Return or Read Receipt," follow the same steps listed above to delay delivery. But, this time, uncheck the box for "Do not deliver before" and instead select one of the checkboxes in the section above for "Request a delivery receipt for this message" or "Request a read receipt for this message." The first one will notify you once the message has been successfully delivered to the recipient's inbox, regardless of whether they open it or not. The second one will notify you when the recipient has opened the message so long as the recipient allows such notification (many users will not allow a return receipt to be sent).

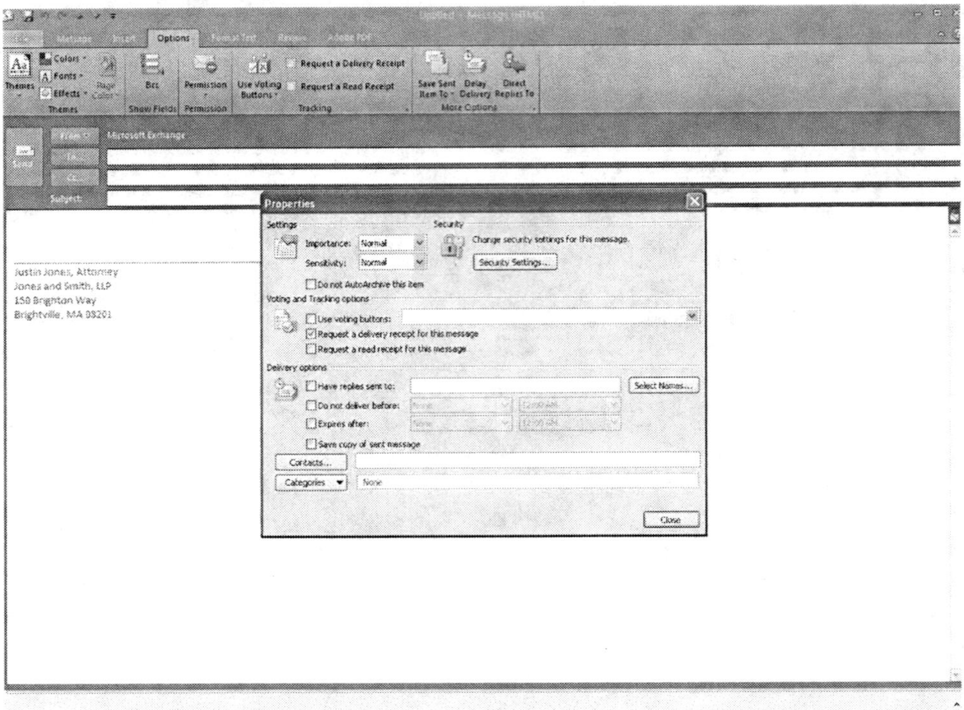

[3] Setting Custom Auto-Signatures for Different Types of Correspondence

Adding a signature line to your email is a smart way to identify yourself, your firm or company, and your contact details should the recipient of your message prefer to phone you, write you by mail, send you a fax, or print your message and have your email address handy when they are away from their main computer.

The nature of our work as legal professionals today often involves taking on different roles in and outside our offices. We may serve as the head of the Litigation Department while also serving as the Pro-bono Coordinator. We may work as an Associate Attorney while moonlighting as an Adjunct Law Professor. Or we may send both professional and personal emails from the same Outlook server. In any of these instances, we should consider using a unique signature for different purposes.

The screenshots below show you how to add a signature to your Outlook signature file and then how to select it for your correspondence.

STEP 1: Begin a new email message. Select the tab or ribbon labeled "Signature" to open the signatures file.

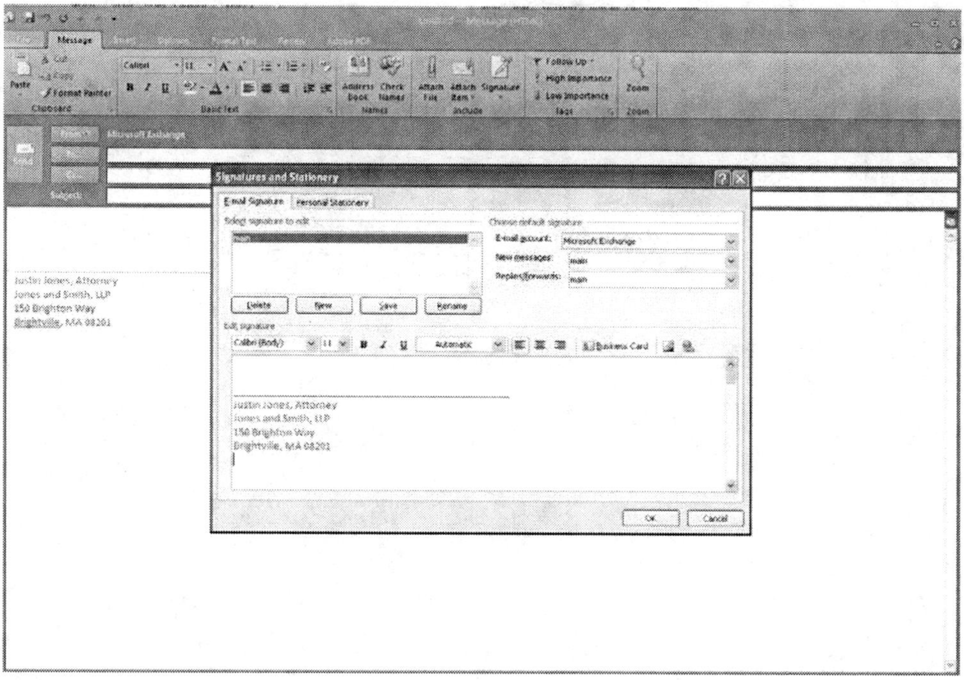

STEP 2: Next, click the "New" button to create a new signature that will be used for different types of correspondence or with a different email account (if you have multiple accounts set-up with a single Outlook server). Name your new signature something that associates it with the purpose. Insert your signature into the white text box and adjust the font as you wish (this will be the font used for your message body when you write emails as well, so make them consistent). Then select "Save."

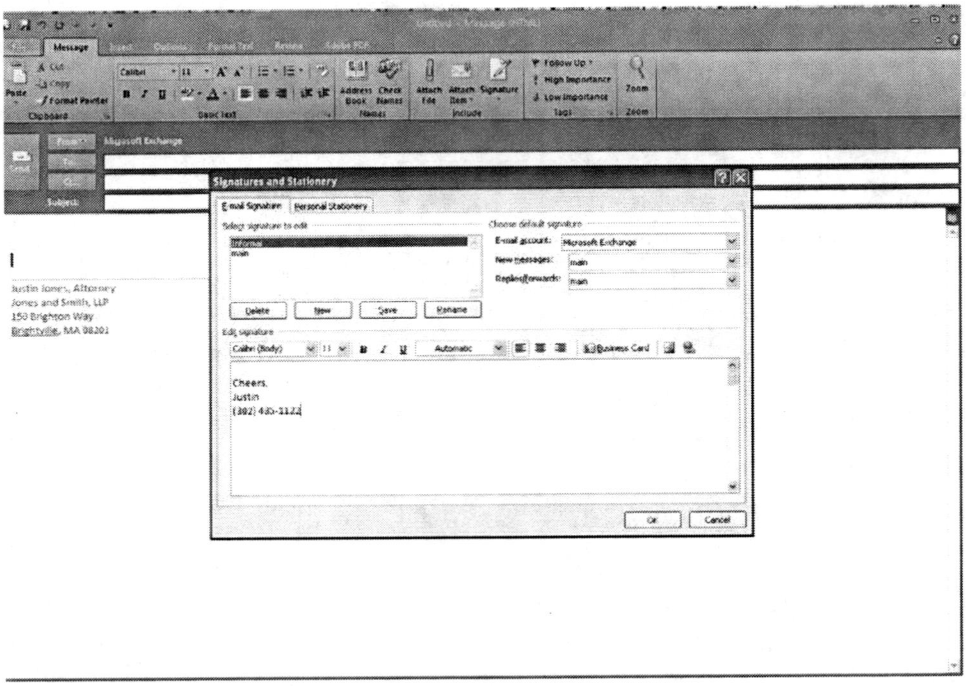

In this case, I have named my new signature "Informal," intending to use it for personal communications with friends.

STEP 3 (If using multiple email accounts): One of the advantages of Outlook is that it allows you to integrate numerous email accounts into a single platform. This means that you can have your office email and personal email all arrive via the same email program. If you do this, you will want to associate the correct signature with the correct account. Once you do this quick adjustment, every time you draft an email or respond to an email from a certain account, the signature associated with that account will automatically appear in the message body.

To associate signatures with accounts, continuing from where we left off in Step 2, simply select the "Email account" pull-down menu on the right of the screen and select the account you want to associate with a signature. Then select the menu below that for "New messages" and select the signature you wish to use for new messages from that account. Finally, do the same for "Replies/ Forwards" for that account. Then click "Save." You are all done.

Note that if you are in the midst of typing an email and you wish to change your signature for that particular message, you do not need to go through all this again. Simply right-click on the signature and select the one that you wish to use.

[F] A FEW CLOSING THOUGHTS ON TECHNOLOGY IN THE LEGAL PROFESSION

With all good things come risks. This is quite true with the advent of new technology. From iPads and iPhones to custom-designed software and apps for lawyers, we have a wide selection of goodies to choose from to enhance access to and organization of our work. With a substantial number of lawyers and legal assistants in the United States today, the market is ripe with opportunity for technology developers. Yet these tools, while flashy on the outside, may increase the potential for user error.

One example of the potential risk from technology relates to the iPad. The idea of the device as a tool of productivity is to give the user access to emails, files, and other materials while away from the office. Users can take notes, record meetings, and manage their calendar from the device. However, the email tools on the iPad are basic and do not allow for secure attachments, return receipts, unique signatures for multiple accounts, and so forth. The document processing program offers limited functionality and does not allow the user to effectively edit a document, spreadsheet, or presentation. Accordingly, your ability to properly modify documents, respond effectively to clients or colleagues, and maintain confidentiality in electronic communications may be inhibited by the device.

However, the convenience of having this technology available to read messages and documents (without editing them), keep track of appointments, and take meeting notes, among other things, is unmistakable. Thus, take this only as a cautionary reminder that technology enhances our access, but creates (or fails to overcome) potentially harmful situations.

Chapter 5

DRAFTING LEGAL MEMORANDA AND CASE BRIEFS

[A] INTRODUCTION

The legal memorandum is to U.S. law firms what the business strategy document is to corporations. It is intended to present a thorough and clear analysis of a particular legal issue and recommend a certain action to be taken. In general, your audience for a legal memorandum will be other legal practitioners, which means that the substance of your writing is especially crucial if your advice is to be heeded.

Topics Covered in This Chapter:

- Stating the Issue in a Proper Opening
- Developing an Outline
- Sections and Headings
- Advanced Paragraph and Section Transitions
- Avoiding Redundancy
- Being Succinctly Detailed
- Applying Sources

[B] THE LEGAL MEMORANDUM

A legal memorandum is a predictive document designed to evaluate a particular issue, client, or case and makes recommendations on the anticipated outcome based on existing law. It is a comprehensive document, often consisting of complex legal analysis and assessment of a narrow legal question. And in most cases, it is used as the basis for crafting a brief to the court if the case is accepted and ultimately tried.

Your goal in a legal memorandum is to provide a complete background on the issue, identify and explain all relevant precedent that would likely apply in the case, and present guidance about how the issue would likely be resolved by the court. Accordingly, the legal memo should contain the following elements:

- Headings
- Question Presented
- Short Answer

- Statement of the Facts
- Discussion (e.g., Analysis)
- Conclusion/Recommendations

As with most legal documents, you have some discretion in terms of the titles for each section of the document and their order. However, a legal memorandum would not be complete without each of the elements listed above. A sample memorandum is included in Appendix A for your reference and below is a brief explanation of what each element should include.

[1] Headings

It is a good idea to use a cover page or set aside the upper half of the first page of your legal memorandum for your headings. In this section, you will want to identify the document as either a Memorandum, Memorandum on Points of Law and Authorities, or Legal Memorandum (all refer to the same type of document).

Your next step is to address the memorandum properly. A memorandum is never written with the formalities of correspondence; however, it should have a specific audience in mind. Identify to whom the memorandum is addressed to and their title; who it is from (presumably you) and their title; the subject of the memorandum, which should reference the specific legal issue or client file name and number; and, the date the memorandum was completed. Do not include superfluous information in the heading section.

[2] Question Presented

A carefully drafted question in a legal memo will undoubtedly set apart an outstanding legal writer from a mediocre one. If you were drawing a map to get somewhere, the question presented would be the address of where you are going. If it is drafted properly, you will have no trouble at all getting there. But, if it is hastily drafted or incomplete, you may be wasting valuable time in your analysis.

The question presented is the legal question you are trying to resolve. Every case turns on one or two key legal issues, even if the case is full of minor legal issues. Your question presented highlights that key legal issue in light of controlling precedent or statutes. In other words, it provides you with the address of where you are going, but it also asks whether you will get there given the terrain ahead.

The question presented should be short — no more than one or two sentences — and it should be presented in the form of a question. However, it should not be so short as to leave out the substantive elements that you will be reviewing in the pages following. Some examples of poorly-drafted and well-drafted questions are listed below:

Poorly-drafted questions:

- Is the client guilty of trespass?
- Will Mr. Jones be able to get jurisdiction over the defendant?

- How does this jurisdiction define criminal homicide?

Well-drafted questions:

- Under Pennsylvania's trespass statute, is a person liable for damages when they were pushed onto the property of another by force?
- Do New York courts grant personal jurisdiction over a defendant who spends his summers in New York but has taken no affirmative steps to change his residency?
- Does Massachusetts's law define criminal homicide to include offenses by minors at the direction of their adult parents?

As you can see from these examples, the question presented is short, yet detailed enough to alert the reader to the particular aspect of the case that will be determine whether the client succeeds or fails. Overlooking or misstating the key issue will lead you to provide the wrong analysis and thus the wrong advice.

[3] Short Answer

The short answer is exactly what it says it is. You are providing the answer before you give the analysis. Of course, you cannot reasonably write this section of the memo before completing the legal analysis below. However, this short answer should be placed immediately after the question presented so that the reader has a quick question and answer up front and can then determine whether they wish to continue with the analysis.

Your short answer should always include the key reason that supports the answer to your question. It should never be "yes" or "no" alone. Consider the following examples of effective short answers:

- Courts in this jurisdiction have consistently ruled that intent is not a required element to prove trespass, making it unlikely for our client to prevail in this case.
- Past precedent in New York suggests that jurisdiction could not be found for temporary visitors; however, more recent cases have allowed exceptions for lengthier stays. Jurisdiction in our case is possible, but not certain.
- No. According to Massachusetts Code § 101.1, minors are excluded from the definition of criminal homicide and must be tried under the Juvenile Offenses Act.

Each of these short answers gives just enough information to make an informed decision, without burdening the reader with extensive analysis. However, the answer could not have been crafted without performing a thorough legal analysis and most lawyers reviewing legal memoranda should be expected to review that analysis carefully.

[4] Statement of the Facts

The statement of the facts refers to the relevant and background facts only. Relevant facts are facts that have a bearing on the legal outcome of the case. Background facts are facts that relate to the legal outcome of the case but do not necessarily affect that outcome. All of this information should be presented in the fact statement in a neutral tone (you are not trying to convince the reader of anything here).

What you should be sure to discard are irrelevant facts — facts that have no relevance to or bearing on the legal outcome of the case. A typical client will present you with all the facts that they have, not knowing which ones will impact their potential case. Your job is to sift through those facts to weed out unnecessary information.

If there is any procedural history to the case (i.e., you are considering an appeal from an unfavorable trial court decision), include that in this section as well. Explain the outcome of the lower courts and, in one or two sentences, why they ruled against your client. Again, do this in a neutral manner.

Be sure not to raise any legal arguments in this section. Save those for the discussion that follows. Your facts section should give the story of the case, but nothing more.

[5] Discussion

The discussion section of your legal memo is the where you will begin your legal analysis. Here, you want to begin by expanding on the question that you presented above. What is it that you are asking and why is that the key issue? What role does the statute or key precedent that you found play in resolving that question? And what related questions are easily answered by the law that you are applying in the case (so that we may dispose of them quickly)?

The first thing you will need to do is to break down the rule that you plan to use, whether it is a statute, case, regulation, or set of cases. Every rule consists of a set of elements. Use those elements to guide your discussion, setting each one apart in a new subsection of the discussion. Be sure to note the connection between the elements in the rule. It will generally fall into one of the following categories:

- Conjunctive: every element of the rule is required in order for it to be applied.
- Disjunctive: at least one element of the rule is required in order for it to be applied.
- Factor or balancing test: the more elements of the rule that are met, the more likely it is that the rule will be applied.

How each element is connected to the rule will control how your analysis of each element fits into the rule and how you structure that analysis. For example, if you have a disjunctive rule, you may want to start with an analysis of the factor that you clearly have, which should make the remainder of the analysis less critical to the outcome.

Once you have identified each of the elements in the rule and how they are connected to one another, take each on one its own and establish a research strategy for that element. Your goal is to identify the relevant statutes, case law, regulations, and other jurisprudence that defines and explains that element. You are not looking for an all-encompassing analysis of the theoretical foundations of the element. Rather, you are searching for an explanation of the element in the context of your case.

To do this, I suggest something akin to the following as a research strategy:

1. Learn about the element in plain English. Use secondary sources or, as a starting place, Google to give you sources that explain the relevance of the element and its evolution. Keep in mind that none of what you find in this first step will be recorded in the brief. This is for you to get your mind around the element to make you a more effective researcher.
   a. If you are already familiar with the element, use this as a refresher to review the latest news or analysis of the element. Spend no more than an hour doing so.
   b. If this is a new element to you or one you have not used in a long time, read several distinct sources to give you a framework within which to define the element. Spend two or three hours in this process.
2. Conduct a broad statutory and case law search. Based on the knowledge that you attained from step one, craft a set of search terms that broadly outlines the element and would capture even tangentially related jurisprudence. If you have access to a legal database such as LexisNexis, run your search here using a jurisdiction specific search (selecting the jurisdiction you plan to bring the case in). If you do not have access to a legal database, run the search in Google Scholar adding the name of the state in which you wish to acquire jurisdiction.
3. If you have a manageable number of cases to briefly review at this point (e.g., fewer than 50), then begin skimming them to identify specifically what the court said about the element you searched for. Highlight this or jot it down on a notepad with the citation for the case. If you still have too many cases, add an additional term to your search to narrow it further. You can also limit it by date to retrieve only cases in the last ten years, for instance.
4. At the end of this process, you should have a long list of cases that have addressed the element and you should start seeing opinions that refer to other cases that you have already come across. This is a sign that you are reaching the end of your case law search for this element. Once you run out of "new" analyses by the courts of your element, you can stop the search.
5. Be mindful of any statutes, regulations, or advisory opinions on point. These will usually be referenced in the cases that you identify; however, newer statutes and regulations may not have had an opportunity to be tried in the courts yet, so run a search with the same search terms for statutes and regulations in the jurisdiction where you plan to file suit.

6. Next, rank your cases by their weight, placing opinions with the most precedential value on top and those with least on the bottom. Make note of the dates of the decisions to ensure that you have the latest analysis.

7. And finally, validate your authority. In LexisNexis, you would do this with the Shepard's function, which tells you if the cases you plan to rely upon have been questioned, criticized, overturned, or supported by other courts. There is no equivalent online mechanism outside legal databases to perform this validation.

For more tips on legal research techniques, see Kevin J. Fandl, *Narrowing the Gap: Legal English for the New International Legal Practitioner* (ABA 2012).

The legal research process is lengthy and can be quite expensive if a legal database is used. The tips above are meant to focus your search and help you to quickly identify the most relevant authorities to support your analysis. However, bear in mind that complex cases may require more extensive searches as well as the use of persuasive authority from other jurisdictions. That is beyond the scope of this text.

Now that you have identified the relevant case law and statutes that interpret the element you are interested in within the context of your case, you can begin to present the analysis. Begin with the lead case or statute — usually a case or statute that provides a clear definition for the element. For example:

> The Pennsylvania Supreme Court defined the element of "dwelling" to include any non-movable structure in which residents received their meals and slept most nights. *See Albert v. Zoning Hearing Bd. of North Abington Tp.*, 578 Pa. 439, 445 (2004).

This hypothetical definition of "dwelling" will inform the remainder of our analysis of whether a client accused of burglary (among other things) was in fact entering the "dwelling of another." Leading with a case from the highest court in the jurisdiction, assuming it is still good law, is an effective way to set the tone for the rest of the analysis. The rest of the analysis will support and clarify this definition, lending it the particularity that you will need to link or distinguish the element from your client's actions.

There are two approaches to drafting the discussion section of a legal memo: (1) leading each paragraph with a new case that speaks to one or more of the elements; or, (2) leading each paragraph with a refined analysis of the element supported by one or more cases. In my experience, the latter approach is more effective at providing clear and convincing evidence to support the ultimate conclusion.

Each paragraph in your memorandum, following the second approach, should look something like the following:

Sentence 1: Definition or clarification of the element.

> Example: Most courts in this jurisdiction have held that a motor home is not a dwelling within the legal meaning of "burglary."

Sentences 2-3: Supporting analysis of the thesis sentence.

> Example: In *Jones v. Smith*, the court found that a motor home used occasionally for vacations was not a dwelling because usage was sporadic. [citation]. In *Holmes v. Nugent*, the court held that a conversion van with a bed and small kitchen used for week-long business trips was not a dwelling because the owner maintained a residence elsewhere. [citation].

Sentences 4-5 (if necessary): Conflicting evidence that may question the thesis sentence.

> Example: However, in *Sandy v. Shore*, the court concluded that a motor home that was parked permanently in a trailer park and used for eating and sleeping every day was a "dwelling" within the meaning of the law. [citation].

Final Sentence: Preliminary application of the analysis to your case.

> Exercise: In our case, the client maintained a residence in addition to his motor home and did not spend more than two weeks at a time in the motor home.

If your analysis is more complex, you may wish to use full paragraphs for each of the points listed above. However, your sequence should be the same: (1) identify the rule; (2) support and clarify the rule with applicable cases; and (3) provide a preliminary conclusion based upon the facts of your case. Repeat this process for each element of the rule, paying close attention to the connection between each element.

[6] Conclusion/Recommendations

Your conclusion should be concise and based clearly upon the analysis that you already performed. The goal here is to take each of the preliminary conclusions that you drafted at the end of your discussion of each element, and formulate a single final conclusion in sync with those findings.

A few things to note in the conclusion section:

- Do not begin any new arguments or introduce any new jurisprudence here.
- Do not state the conclusion with absolute certainty — there is always room for doubt.

Your conclusion should leave the reader feeling like you have successfully glued all of the elements together and made your recommendation undeniable. Whether you have concluded that your client will win or lose their case, your logic must be clear and sound. Your recommendation will likely be relied upon to take (or avoid) legal action. Incomplete or incorrect guidance can cost the firm financially and may affect their reputation overall.

Rest assured that if you have performed your analysis thoroughly and have followed the logical approach outlined above, you can feel confident in your guidance. Legal professionals in the United States have applied this approach for many years and have come to rely upon the simple logic that it offers. Applying it in your own drafting will help to make you a more effective legal writer.

EXERCISE, PART 1: FRAMING THE ISSUE

Review the set of facts below, which you noted during an interview with a potential client. Rewrite the facts in the form of a legal issue and predict the potential outcome if your firm agrees to take on this client. Insert references to fictitious law as needed.

Exercise 1: Client: Michael Johnson

Interview Date: April 12, 2012

Facts:

Johnson acquired the Picasso painting, *Last Realm*, in 1995 for the price of $1.5 million. Johnson was divorced in 2008 and needed to sell the Picasso painting to pay half of the value of the asset to his ex-wife in the divorce settlement.

Johnson delivered the painting to Sam Beekman, an art dealer, at Beekman's store on December 1, 2009, to sell on consignment. Beekman filed for Chapter 7 bankruptcy on January 1, 2010. Beekman's creditors claim all assets in Beekman's "inventory" at his store are part of the bankruptcy case and are able to be sold to cover Beekman's debts. Johnson stated that he believed that most of the items Beekman was displaying in his store were on consignment. Johnson wants the Picasso painting back to sell to another art dealer, and does not want to become part of Beekman's bankruptcy case."

Sample answer can be found in Appendix A.

Exercise 2: Client: Lucie Lockett

Review the following fact statement from your client, Lucie Lockett. Identify the legal issue in the case and determine who would be the proper defendants. Then, in part 2, using the sources of law following the case, determine which court and in what state the suit should be brought.

Interview Date: March 23, 2012

Facts:

Lockett went to a pet store called *Tropics North* in her home town of Silver Spring, Maryland, on September 20, 2011, to buy a pet snake for her brother for his 12th birthday. She was interested in one bright green snake, and asked the sales clerk to hold it. The sales clerk brought her to the back of the store and allowed her to "pet" the snake and pick it up. After "a minute or two" of holding the snake, the snake bit her three times on the arm. She had to go to the hospital in an ambulance.

She found out that the snake in the Maryland store came from an exotic pet supplier in Miami, Florida, which supplies many of the store's exotic pets. The pet store owner in Maryland, George McConnell, disclaims responsibility based upon posted signs in the store stating that the store is not responsible for any injuries resulting from handling the animals in the store. Lockett would like to pursue her case against both the pet store and the Miami pet store supplier.

Lockett has incurred $20,000 in hospital expenses. It is projected that she will spend $6,480 for physical therapy over the next six months. She has been unable to work for the last two months resulting in $1,440 in lost wages from her job as a reporter. It is likely she will not be able to work while she is in physical therapy which will result in additional lost wages in the amount of $4,320. She will need at least two additional surgeries estimated to be at least $10,000 each. The diminished value of her arm may be $374,400 (the amount of lost wages if she is unable to work full-time as a result of her weakened arm and retires at age 65). The total amount of damages is $426,640 and does not take into account pain and suffering.

Sample answer can be found in Appendix A.

EXERCISE, PART 2: APPLYING SOURCES OF LAW

After you have successfully extracted the legal issue from the fact statement or interview with the client, your next step is to begin looking for sources of law that explain and outline the parameters of that legal issue. Your goal in this next step is to develop a comprehensive understanding of the intricacies of the legal issue and how courts have addressed it in your jurisdiction and other jurisdictions.

In this exercise, you have uncovered eight potentially valuable sources of law addressing the issue raised by the Lockett fact pattern above. Review each source and assess whether it would be valuable or not in drafting your legal memorandum. Be sure to consider the jurisdiction, date decided, and issue addressed by each case.

(1.) *Heath v. Swift Wings*, 252 S.E.2d 526 (N.C. App. 1979): Holding: (1) an instruction defining negligence by referring to the "ordinary care and caution," which an ordinary prudent pilot having the same training and experience as a "pilot of the plane would have used in the same or similar circumstances," was erroneous; (2) the evidence did not reasonably support the trial court's statement that the pilot had initiated emergency procedures; and (3) there was no basis for the trial court's statement that the administrator insisted that the pilot adhere to a perfect standard of care as opposed to a reasonable standard of care.

(2.) *International Shoe Co. v. Washington*, 326 U.S. 310, 320 (1945): Holding: Due process of law" requires only that in order to subject a defendant to a judgment *in personam*, if he be not present within territory of forum, he has certain minimum contacts with it such that maintenance of the suit does not offend traditional notions of fair play and substantial justice. The demand that corporation be "present" in state to satisfy due process of law requirement for purpose of maintenance of suit against it in courts of state may be met by such contacts of corporation with the state of forum as make it reasonable, in context of federal system of government, to require corporation to defend the particular suit which is brought there, and an "estimate of inconveniences" which would result to corporation from a trial away from its "home" or principal place of business would be relevant in such connection.

(3.) *Ortiz v. Animal Exotique Boutique*, 66 A.2d 587 (MD 2011): Holding: Snake was not considered exotic animal under state liability statute and thus snake owner could only be found liable for regular damages that were foreseeable from standard animal bite.

(4.) *World-Wide Volkswagen Corp. v. Woodson*, 444 U.S. 286 (1980): Holding where corporate defendants, automobile wholesaler and retailer, carried on no activity whatsoever in Oklahoma and availed themselves of no privileges or benefits of

Oklahoma law, mere fortuitous circumstance that a single automobile sold in New York to New York residents happened to suffer an accident while passing through Oklahoma did not constitute "minimum contacts" with Oklahoma so as to permit Oklahoma courts to exercise jurisdiction consistently with due process under state long-arm statute interpreted by Oklahoma courts as conferring jurisdiction to limits permitted by United States Constitution.

(5.) *Haggard v. Ritsick*, 47 N.E.2d 33 (Mass. 2009): Holding: Pet store owner not liable to customer for exotic snake biting customer because pet store posted signs limiting their liability that the store would not be liable for any injuries from exposure to pets.

(6.) *Asahi Metal Industry v. Superior Court*, 480 U.S. 102 (1987): Holding that exercise of jurisdiction by a California court over a Japanese manufacturer would be unreasonable and unfair where the Japanese manufacturer took no active steps to engage in commerce in California. A substantial connection between the defendant and the forum state is necessary to establish minimum contact and this connection must come about by purposeful action of the defendant directed toward forum state. The fact that the manufacturer knew that its parts would be used in goods sold in California is not sufficient to establish minimum contact in that state.

(7.) *Burger King Corp. v. Rudzewicz*, 471 U.S. 462 (1985): A franchisor in Florida brought action in Florida courts against a Michigan franchisee alleging breach of contract obligations and trademark infringement. The Michigan party argued lack of personal jurisdiction because the party had only limited contact with Florida. The Court held that the franchisee agreed to jurisdiction via the contract documents and that they were given fair notice of potential litigation in Florida. Accordingly, the franchisee established a "substantial and continuing" presence with the state of Florida. The due process clause of the Fourteenth Amendment protects an individual's liberty in not being subject to the binding judgments of a forum with which he has established no meaningful contacts, ties, or relations; however, franchisee in this case failed to establish that jurisdiction in Florida would be fundamentally unfair.

(8.) *Iguana Pet Store v. State of Florida*, 55 So.3d 1475 (Fla. Dist. Ct. App. 2010): Holding the Florida Statute § 372.90 was developed to regulate the transportation of exotic pets and it is illegal to ship exotic pets without prior approval of registration application through the Department of Natural Resources, Conservation, Reclamation and Use.

Suggested answers can be found in Appendix A.

[C] CLOSING THOUGHTS ON LEGAL MEMORANDA

Below are some questions to ask when you draft a legal memorandum:

- Identifying the issue
  - What is the central question you need answered?
  - Are there related questions that should be addressed?

    - What led to the question in the first place?
- Framing the issue
    - Have you kept your issue statement short?
    - Is your issue statement persuasive?
    - Does your issue statement recommend a certain outcome?
- Supporting the issue
    - Is your issue supported by foundational statements?
    - Is your issue free of opinionated statements?
- Analyzing the issue
    - Have you applied inductive reasoning to establish a rule?
    - Have you outlined the rule?
    - Have you applied the rule to your issue?
- Concluding
    - Does your conclusion logically follow your analysis?

[D] CASE BRIEFS

A case brief is a short summary or abstract of a case that has already been decided. These are relied on extensively by law students and less frequently by practitioners when conducting legal research. A case brief serves to inform the reader in an efficient manner the key elements of the case that they would need to know to explain it to a third party, analyze it in light of a particular client's facts, or factor it into a legal memorandum.

A typical case brief should be no more than one page. Highly complex cases involving numerous issues of law may require an additional page. However, more than two pages eliminate the key function of a case brief — to provide an efficient overview of a case.

A case brief should be prepared whenever you or another party needs quick access to the information in the case, or in the event that you will likely reference this case again in future legal memoranda. Having a database of well-written case briefs can be a valuable time-saving tool. If you keep them organized properly on your computer or in your files, you will be able to quickly refresh your memory of the case and determine whether it will help you in your future legal research projects.

The elements of a case brief are relatively standard. And like the legal memorandum, you have some flexibility in how you organize those elements. It is wise to adopt a method that is comfortable for you and others who read your briefs and to maintain that method for consistency. In general, you will want to include the following elements in a case brief:

- Parties/Case Citation
- Facts and Procedural History
- Issues
- Decision/Holding
- Reasoning
- Separate opinions (if applicable)
- Analysis

How will you fit all of that information on one page? By using short, substantive sentences. This is an excellent learning tool for legal writers who tend to write in a verbose manner, using more words than necessary to convey a point. The case brief is meant to be highly condensed and to give the reader only the information that is essential to their understanding of the case.

[1] Parties/Case Citation

At the top of your case brief, you should include the names of the parties and the citation of the case. Only use the last names of the parties and try to write the citation in Bluebook format so that it is easily transferred to the legal memorandum or court briefs later. Also, be sure that you are briefing the most recent case. In LexisNexis, you can confirm this by clicking the "Shepardize" button, which will show you where the citation you are using fits into the procedural history of the case.

When you refer to the parties throughout the brief, it is wise to refer to them by their court designation:

- Trial court designations: Plaintiff vs. Defendant
- Appellate court designations: Appellant vs. Appellee
- Supreme Court designations: Petitioner vs. Respondent

The first party listed in the name of the case will always be the Plaintiff, Appellant, or Petitioner. The second party listed will always be the Defendant, Appellee, or Respondent. However, these designations may change on appeal, so do not assume that the Appellant on appeal was also the Plaintiff at the trial court.

The citation is the address of the case in a reporter. A reporter is a paperback or online book where all published cases can be found. Most cases will have multiple citations because they are published in multiple reporters. These are known as parallel citations. Although courts still use these in their opinions sometimes, it is not usually necessary to include parallel citations in your case briefs or in your legal memoranda. The first citation following the party names is sufficient to find the case in a paperback or online reporter (or in Google).

[2] Facts/Procedural History

Just as with the legal memorandum, the facts of a case brief should be very short. The process is a bit easier for briefs because you are extracting facts from a court opinion that has already condensed the facts substantially from the trial. Unlike in a memo, where you need to sift through a client's facts to determine which ones are relevant, the court has done that work for you. However, you must still be selective in which facts you include in the brief so that don't get lost in unnecessary details.

Your statement of the facts should be one short paragraph in length in the brief. The words should be your own — not the words of the court. This ensures that you understand the facts of the case and can easily explain them in the context of the legal argument being made. Your focus should be on the complaint and the reason it was filed in the first place, which will come forth in the fact statement of the court's opinion.

You should also include in this section a brief procedural history. This could be as simple as saying that the case is an appeal from an unfavorable trial court ruling against the current appellant, or it may be a slightly lengthier explanation of the motions that led to the current procedural posture of the case. In no case should this section exceed two sentences.

[3] Issues

The issue is the central legal question in the case that the court was asked to address. In many cases, the court explicitly states the issue at the outset, usually following the facts and procedural history of the case. In some cases, however, it is less clear and requires you to sift through the language of the court to find the question they are addressing.

If possible, state the issue as a question that can be answered directly. Consider the following example of an issue statement from the model brief found in Appendix B:

> *Whether the petitions of Gul and Hamad, appellants, are not moot and whether the district court made certain procedural errors in reaching the contrary conclusion?*

With an issue presented in this manner, the analysis and holding can be easily linked-up to the question, giving you a straightforward outline of the case. In this example, the case turns on whether the court below made procedural errors. In other cases, the court may consider whether a particular statute applies, or whether an exception can be carved out from a provision of law. In all of these cases, framing the issue as a question will help you to identify the answer.

[4] Decision/Holding

The holding of the court is quite simply how it ruled in this case. How did it answer the question that you posed in the previous section — affirmatively or negatively? This section can be as short as a few words, such as:

The court affirmed the lower court's decision.

However, it is better to include enough detail to link the decision to the question presented:

> *The court affirmed the lower court's decision denying personal jurisdiction where defendant had no substantial contact with the state.*

[5] Reasoning

Some lawyers combine the holding with the reasoning/analysis section for brevity. That is a matter of preference.

The reasoning section describes the analysis the court conducted in reaching their decision. This section should only include the analysis performed by the majority if it is a split decision. In this section, you will go into more detail about the key cases or statutes the court relied upon in reaching their decision, and any factors that stood out as particularly relevant in the analysis. Keep the following questions in mind when drafting the reasoning section, all the while remembering to keep this to one or two paragraphs:

1. What did the court hold?
2. What did the court base their holding on?
3. Why did the court apply that law/case as opposed to others?
4. What factors did the court highlight in their analysis?
5. If the court established a new legal test or definition, what is it?

[6] Separate Opinions

In split decisions, some judges join the majority opinion and others either concur or dissent. The dissent and concurrence should be noted, but only briefly as they are not part of the precedent created by this decision. Each separate concurrence or dissent should be explained in one sentence.

> Concurring Opinion: the judge agrees with the outcome of the majority decision but not with the analysis used to reach that outcome.
>
> Dissenting Opinion: the judge disagrees with the outcome and the analysis used to reach that outcome by the majority.

[7] Analysis

The final analysis section is distinct from the reasoning described above in that this section focused on the impact of the decision on the public at large or other cases in particular. Your goal in this section, if you see a need to include it in your brief, is to describe the significance of this case in the overall field of law and policy in your own words. You would especially want to include this section when the case:

- Changes a previously accepted approach to something;

- Overturns a significant law or questions a line of cases; or
- Holds a law unconstitutional.

Examples of Case Briefs can be found in Appendix B.

Chapter 6

DRAFTING CONTRACTS

[A] INTRODUCTION

A contract is a unique animal in legal writing and you will need to apply a different set of rules to it from most other types of legal writing. Every word creates potential liability for a client, and misinterpretations can ultimately lead to court challenges requiring additional funds and delaying achievement of your client's goals. We will focus on precision and careful drafting above all else in this section.

Topics Covered in This Chapter:

- Discerning the Purpose of the Contract
- Developing the Recitals
- How your Client's Strategy Affects the Sequence of Clauses
- Key Clauses
- Optional Clauses
- Choice of Law/Forum

[B] THE IMPORTANCE OF EFFECTIVE CONTRACT DRAFTING SKILLS

- Not the same as basic legal skills
- Not the same as litigation skills
- Preparing your client for the unexpected
- Providing your client with security

A contract attorney is a unique type of attorney. In general, they are very detail-oriented, meticulous, and systematic. Drafting contracts is an art and requires an artist with sufficient understanding of the details of the transaction along with an ability to foresee risks and potential disputes before the contract is even drafted. An effective contract drafting attorney is a litigator's best friend in the firm as they give them the strongest possible case to make in favor of their shared client.

This also means that contract drafting attorneys are not creative drafters — at least not when drafting contracts for clients. They often prefer using language in the contract that has stood up to challenges in court and that provides the best protection for their client. Many clauses are used similarly in multiple contracts, but a good contract drafter will always customize the clause to the specific situation.

Regardless of whether you draft contracts for a living, most of what we do in the world today has some connection to contracts, whether we are ordering a new pair of shoes off the Internet or entering a multi-year distribution agreement. Because of this, it is critical for all legal professionals to develop the skills necessary to put together and understand an effective contract and to recognize the potential for a contract dispute by simply reading the contract language. This chapter aims to educate that broader group of legal professionals who, while it may not be their full-time job, have some exposure to contracts in their legal career.

In this chapter, we will review some of the common mistakes in drafting contracts and highlight effective language for certain standard clauses. Every contract is unique and includes new or different clauses; however, some procedural clauses exist in almost every contract, so we will focus on those.

- Types of Contract Language
- The Front of the Contract
- The Body of the Contract
- The Back of the Contract
- Drafting Pointers

[C] LETTERS OF INTENT

A letter of intent is a preliminary document meant to express the parties' desire to do business together (i.e., to enter into a binding contract with one another). This letter is often necessary to secure financing to support one or both of the parties and may be used for approval from governmental entities to secure licenses and other essential facets of the deal. The letter of intent is not intended to be part of the contract, which is drafted and entered into subsequently.

A letter of intent or agreement is usually necessary in international transactions and, if properly drafted, serves only as an indication of what the parties may do in the future:

> "Agreements to agree" are generally unenforceable because they provide neither a basis for determining the existence of a breach nor for giving an appropriate remedy."[26]

But note that these "agreements to agree" may create an obligation for the party to act in good faith in their execution of the terms of that agreement. A court in California explained it as:

---

[26] *Richie Co., LLP v. Lyndon Ins. Group, Inc.*, 316 F.3d 748 (8th Cir. 2003).

> A party will be liable only if a failure to reach ultimate agreement resulted from a breach of that party's obligation to negotiate or to negotiate in good faith.[27]

However, a poorly drafted letter of intent can create serious problems for your clients by establishing itself as a binding contract. Consider this recent case from Delaware, which addressed a letter of intent that contained a confidentiality provision that was ultimately breached by the defendant:

> "Sufficiently definite" letters of intent can create enforceable obligations. If the parties do not wish to be bound by a LOI, they "can readily do that by expressly saying that the letter of intent is nonbinding." In addition, "parties enter into letters of intent for a reason. They don't enter into them . . . [to] be disregarded whenever situations change. They enter into them because they create rights."[28]

For this reason, drafting a letter of intent should be done very carefully, noting exactly what the parties intend and are willing to be bound to perform during the pre-contract stage. Pay close attention to the case law in the jurisdiction where the parties are located to assess how those courts treat letters of intent. And if your client insists that the letter should be non-binding, be sure to include explicit language in the letter to that effect.

A Sample Letter of Intent can be found in Appendix B.

[D] TYPES OF CONTRACT LANGUAGE

Once you have drafted and sent out your letter of intent or agreement, and after the parties have agreed to go forward with the contract, you are ready to begin drafting the contract language. Unlike legal memoranda, which are written to predict the outcome of a case or resolution of an issue, and unlike court briefs and demand letters, which are written to persuade someone to take a certain position, contract language is meant to create obligations and prevent certain acts. Some legal writers call this "preventive writing,"[29] though this may not capture the essence of contract language.

Regardless of the name you assign to it, contract drafting style is very rigid and requires the drafter to be highly selective in their choice of language. A misplaced word or clause, or a provision that assigns responsibility to the wrong party, can lead not only to disputes between the parties, but suits against the lawyers that draft the contract as well.

In a recent example, the law firm of Latham and Watkins was sued by ECC Capital Corporation ("ECC") for improperly drafting a contract between ECC Capital and Bear Stearns & Company. In the complaint, ECC stated: "As a result of Latham and Manatt's incompetent draftsmanship, [Bear Stearns subsidiaries] asserted positions

---

[27] *Copeland v. Baskin Robbins*, 96 Cal. App. 4th 1251, 1257 (2002).

[28] *Global Asset Capital, LLC v. Rubicon US Reit, Inc.*, C.A. No. 5071-VCL (Del. Ch. Nov. 16, 2009).

[29] Nadia Nedzel, *Legal Reasoning, Research and Writing for International Graduate Students*, at 299 (2008).

that would have been untenable under properly drafted transactional documents, including refusing timely to purchase over $1 billion of loans."[30] The importance of proper drafting cannot be overstated.

In a contract, language tends to fall within one of three categories:

<u>Language of Performance</u> — these are clauses written to compel an action. They often include the word "hereby" to indicate that the action is agreed upon by virtue of the contract language.

Example: Company hereby grants the exclusive right to Buyer.

<u>Language of Obligation</u> — these clauses create an obligation on one of the parties to the contract. They are always written in the active voice and generally include the word "must" or "will." Note that "shall," while frequently used in contracts, is discouraged by some drafters as it has been interpreted by some courts as language of discretion.[31] Although the debate over whether to eliminate "shall" from legal documents continues, in contract drafting, it is still widely accepted that the use (but not overuse) of "shall" is appropriate.

Example: Buyer must deliver the payment no later than 30 days following receipt of the goods.

Example: Seller shall not release the funds until Buyer has provided written authorization to do so.

<u>Language of Policy</u> — these clauses are statements of fact that do not intend to create obligations on either party. They are frequently used for contract elements such as establishing the dispute resolution process, setting interest or exchange rates, or setting expiration dates for the exercise of options or conditional clauses. They should be drafted in the present tense and should not include any words creating an obligation, such as "shall" or "must."

> Example: All disputes arising out of this agreement will be resolved by the courts of the state of New York.
>
> Example: Payments received after 30 days following their due date are subject to an interest rate of 5% per day.

Every clause that you draft will be in one of these three forms. Be certain that each clause is drafted in such a way as to achieve the desired result.

[1] Language of Obligation/Discretion

Below are some examples of language of obligation, followed by a brief explanation of the impact of each statement.

---

[30] Drew Combs, *Mortgage Lender Hits Latham and Manatt with Malpractice Suit*, THE AM LAW DAILY (Jan. 12, 2010), *available at* http://amlawdaily.typepad.com/amlawdaily/2010/01/lathammanattsuit.html (accessed on September 29, 2012).

[31] *See, e.g.*, Bryan Garner, *Shall We Abandon Shall?*, ABA Magazine (August 2012). *But see* Kenneth Adams, *Manual of Style for Contract Drafting*, at 31–41 (2008).

Example 1: Buyer shall be responsible to seller for all damages, both compensatory and punitive, in the event that he/she violates any provision of the contract. [The buyer will have to pay the seller for all damages, both compensatory and punitive, if he/she violates any provision of their contract.]

Example 2: Defendant may be fined up to $1,000 and/or sentenced up to 180 days of imprisonment if found guilty by the trial court of having possessed drug paraphernalia. [The defendant can be fined up to $1,000 or imprisoned for up to 180 days if found guilty, but the judge can choose a lesser sentence.]

Example 3: All items must be returned within thirty days for purchaser to receive full refund. [If the purchaser does not return the item within thirty days from the day of purchase, then he/she will not receive any refund.]

Example 4: The property ownership rights shall transfer to the heir upon the death of the owner. [Pursuant to the owner's will, once the owner of the property dies, the heir will own the property.]

Example 5: The provisions of this Agreement shall be construed and the performance thereof governed in accordance with the laws of the State of New York, USA. [If provisions of the Agreement will be construed in accordance with New York law.]

Example 6: Under Article 21 of the Spanish labor law, covenants not to compete shall not exceed two years for technical professions and six months for all other professions. [Companies can require technical professionals to not compete with their business for up to two years upon their departure from the company, and non-technical professionals for up to six months.]

Example 7: Dissolution of the partnership may occur upon agreement of all parties. [The parties can dissolve their partnership through a mutual agreement.]

Example 8: Pursuant to international maritime law, watercraft must not enter within five miles of any foreign state. [Under penalty of international maritime law, boats are forbidden from entering within five miles of any foreign land.]

Example 9: If you are not the intended recipient of this email, you are hereby notified that disclosing, copying or distributing the contents of this information shall subject you to prosecution under the United States Confidentiality Act. [If you were sent an email and were not supposed to receive it, and then forwarded the email to another party, then you will be prosecuted under the United States Confidentiality Act.]

Example 10: Neither party shall be in default hereunder by reason of any failure or delay in the performance of any obligation under this Agreement where such failure or delay arises out of any cause beyond the reasonable control and without negligence of such party. [Neither party will be liable for a failure or delay of any action required under the Agreement if the failure or delay is a result of any cause outside their reasonable control or is not caused by negligence.]

[E] THE FRONT OF THE CONTRACT

The front of the contract refers to the material prior to the substantive obligations found in the body of the contract. This section will include the name of the contract, an introductory clause, recitals, and a transition sentence.

[1] Contract Title and Introductory Clause

The title to the contract should be clear and sufficiently descriptive to inform the reader of the type of contract the parties have constructed. It usually contains the word "agreement" rather than "contract." Some examples include:

- Merger Agreement
- Asset Purchase Agreement
- Trademark License Agreement

The title should be placed at the top and in the center of the first page and it should be written in all caps. Immediately below the title of the agreement should be the introductory clause. This clause identifies the parties to the contract, their form of existence (i.e., type of business or individual), and usually the date on which the contract becomes effective. An example is below:

> CONSULTING SERVICES AGREEMENT
>
> This consulting services agreement is dated June 1, 2012, and is between ROCKY BALBOA, an individual residing at 555 North Fairmont Street, Lexington, Kentucky, 20092 ("Rocky") and BOX AMERICA, LLC, a New York limited liability company ("Boxam").

A few things to keep in mind when drafting the introductory clause:

- If you plan to have the signatories include a date next to their signature, or if you have an effective date elsewhere in the contract, do not include a date in this clause.
- If a party is an individual, provide their full street address and identify them as an "individual."
- If a party is a company, identify their corporate form (e.g., LLC, Inc., S.A.) and place of incorporation.
- Always include a short form for each party name; however, do not use multiple short forms for the same party (e.g., "Company or Party or Firm").

[2] Recitals

The title to the contract should be clear and sufficiently descriptive to inform the reader of the type of contract the parties have constructed. It usually contains the word "agreement" rather than "contract." Some examples include:

The recitals clause in a contract is an optional and preliminary section that explains the purpose for entering the contract. It provides the context for the parties' decision to be bound by the terms of the agreement. In most cases, recitals are not considered binding and are only used if necessary to interpret an ambiguous contract.[32] However, if the recitals are drafted in such a way is to infer intent or expand the performance of the parties, a court may consider them binding.

Recitals should be drafted in plain English, using simple expressions and clear sentences. They should be distinguished from other clauses in the contract so as to avoid associating them with the body of the contract itself. They should describe the purpose for the parties to enter the agreement but should not make any commitments or obligations outside the scope of the contract. An example of an effective recitals clause can be found below:

> BACKGROUND
>
> Rocky and Boxam are parties to a letter of intent, dated November 10, 2011, in which they agreed to assess the viability of formalizing a consulting services agreement.
>
> Boxam wishes to retain the consulting services of Rocky in an effort to recruit and train young athletes for its growing boxing business in New York City. Rocky will interact regularly with boxing trainees at Boxam's locations in Queens and Manhattan.
>
> Rocky and Boxam are parties to a deposit agreement, dated March 1, 2012 ("Deposit Agreement"), in which Boxam agreed to provide a good faith retainer fee of $100,000 to Rocky for his expected services under this agreement.
>
> The parties therefore agree as follows:

A few things to keep in mind when drafting the recitals:

- Use of a heading for this section is optional. However, if a heading is used, do not associate it with an outline number so as to distinguish it from the body of the contract.

[32] *Genovese Drug Stores, Inc. v. Connecticut Packing Co.*, 732 F.2d 286, 291 (2nd Cir. 1983) (holding "an expression of intent in a 'whereas' [recitals] clause of an agreement between two parties may be useful as an aid in construing the rights and obligations created by the agreement, but it cannot create any right beyond those arising from the operative terms of the document.")

- Write in concise but complete sentences.
- If any attachment, exhibit, or schedule is referenced, be sure to provide the short form name for that document and include it by reference in the body of the contract.
- Conclude the recitals with the transition language shown above, which indicates that the following text forms part of the body of the contract. "Therefore" may be substituted with "hereby" as well.

[F] THE BODY OF THE CONTRACT

[1] Defined Terms

In most contracts and in some other legal documents, you will have a need to define one or more terms with a unique, non-standard definition. For instance, rather than using the traditional definition for "coffee beans," you may want to define that term as "whole, unroasted Coffee Beans originating in Colombia." Following your definition of this term, all references in the legal document to "coffee beans" will be associated with that new definition.

The ability to create special meanings for words in a legal document leads some lawyers to define excessively. Bear in mind the following:

- If you plan to associate a word or phrase with its traditional definition (i.e., the dictionary or industry definition), do not include it with your defined terms. This will confuse the reader and will also limit your ability to interpret the word or phrase more broadly.
- If you plan to use a word or phrase both in the standard sense and as a uniquely defined term, consider choosing a different word or phrase for the defined term to avoid confusing it with the standard term. If you must use the same word or phrase, be sure to distinguish the two by capitalizing the defined term and not the standard term.
- If you only use a special definition for a word or phrase only once or twice in the document, consider excluding it from the defined terms section and instead including the definition immediately following the first usage of the word or phrase in the document.

EXERCISE: DEFINED TERMS

Review the following situations and draft a definition for the unique term.

1. Assume you are in-house counsel for a multinational enterprise in negotiations with a foreign state regarding the extraction of their natural resources. You have been tasked with drafting a purchase contract for the rights to an iron mine, and you want to ensure that in the event of contract breach by either party, the claim will be settled through "International Commercial Arbitration." Draft a definition of this term including your jurisdictional venue.

2. Licensor and Distributor seek to enter into an international agreement for the apportionment of an artist's music royalties. Assume you are the artist's attorney, and you must draft the definition of Royalty Income to ensure that your client will collect revenue from the Licensor for retransmission of the client's songs on secondary sources, such as television and the internet, that has been authorized for use by the Licensor to the Distributor.

3. Assume that you are drafting an agreement with third-party subcontractors in a foreign state for security services and want to impose confidentiality requirements on the subcontractors regarding email correspondences. Define Confidential Information in regards to Electronic Delivery.

4. Assume your client has entered into negotiations for an international agreement to buy a banking institution in a historically politically and economically unstable state. Your client wants to protect its interests throughout the negotiation period by having the option to not purchase the bank in the event of a "material adverse change." Define this term.

Suggested solutions can be found in Appendix A.

[2] The Choice of Law/Forum Clause

One of the most important considerations at the outset of drafting a contract is to select the applicable law and legal forum to hear disputes. If both parties reside and do business in the same state, this should not be much of a problem. However, if the parties are from different states or different countries, choice of law can play a significant role in the outcome of future legal disputes.

In general, parties select the law and the court in which disputes over some or all of their contract will be heard. However, it is not quite as easy as selecting a particular law and a particular court and inserting the language into the contract. Much depends on the nature of the parties' business, their locations, and the laws and policies of the jurisdiction selected.

Let's begin our exploration by looking at the key aspects of choice of law and forum clauses — definitions, *forum non-conveniens*, and jurisdiction.

[a] *Choice of Law Clause*

This is the parties' designation of which state's law will govern the interpretation of the contract in the event of a dispute. A party may prefer to select a state where they have some experience or where the laws are particularly favorable to their client. They may also prefer a state in which the law related to the type of transaction is well developed. In many cases, this leads to states such as Delaware, New York, and California being selected for choice of law. Keep in mind, however, that this does not mean that the dispute will be heard in that state.

When selecting the law to apply to the contract, the parties need to consider the relationship of the parties and the transaction to the state from which the law is selected. There are generally two questions courts will ask in this respect before enforcing a choice of law clause:

- Does the state in which the parties have selected their choice of law have a substantial interest in the transaction?
- Do the parties have a reasonable basis for selecting that law?

If both questions are answered negatively, the choice of law clause will likely fail. In this instance, the law of the state that would have jurisdiction over the transaction but for the choice of law clause will likely be applied to the dispute.

[b] *Choice of Forum*

The forum is the seat of the court where the parties wish to have their disputes heard. In other words, this is the geographic location of the court that will hear the case. Parties are free to select any forum they wish, so long as they comply with the procedural rules of that forum. For instance, some courts require the dispute to be above a certain amount of money damages in order for that court to accept the case.

The forum selected can be any court with jurisdiction over the matter in any country, so long as the parties have some reasonable justification for why the dispute should be heard in that forum (see *forum non conveniens* below). If a choice of law clause has also been included, the proper forum will apply the law selected by the parties in the resolution of the dispute. If no choice of law clause was included in the contract, the law of the selected forum will generally apply.

It is wise to select a forum that the parties mutually agree to and that the courts will accept. If there is any indication that the selected forum would be incredibly inconvenient for one party or if the courts in that jurisdiction are corrupt, a court may discard the forum selection clause. Accordingly, the parties should agree on a location that would be acceptable to both parties in the event of a dispute.

[c] Forum Non Conveniens

Forum non conveniens, Latin for "inconvenient forum," is a defense to the selection of a forum to hear a dispute. The defense is raised either by the defendant or *sua sponte* by the court. If successful, the defense will dismiss the case and allow the plaintiff to file again in a more convenient or appropriate forum.

A court may decide to dismiss a case on these grounds for any of the following reasons:

- The parties reside outside the selected forum
- Most of the witnesses and evidence are outside the selected forum
- Public policy
- The burden on the court system

If the court finds that their forum would be inconvenient and the plaintiff has another viable option where he or she can file the claim and potentially win money damages, the case will be dismissed. However, if no other court would have jurisdiction or be able to aware money damages, the court will not dismiss the case on these grounds.

In cross-border cases, courts are likely to take into account the ability of the parties to receive a fair trial in the selected forum. This may come to pass even if the country selected by the parties had a stable and trustworthy judicial system when the contract was signed, but, due to a change in government or other circumstances, the courts are no longer delivering justice. In other cases, the court may dismiss with conditions, including a requirement that a forum jurisdiction use U.S. law as their choice of law.

[3] The Representations and Warranties Clause

The representations and warranties clause is generally used to state factual information about the parties or the circumstances of the contract, in part to give confidence to the other party prior to signing the agreement. These are statements made to induce the other party into the agreement and they are binding on the party making them. Accordingly, they are often the subject of contract disputes. A sample clause is below.

Representations and Warranties of Seller. Seller represents and warrants to Buyer as follows:

1. Seller owns and has good and marketable title to all of the Assets, and as of the Closing date, the Assets are free and clear of all liens, encumbrances, claims, or rights of others or defects in title of any kind whatsoever.
2. Seller has the right, power, legal capacity and authority to enter into and perform the obligations under this Agreement on behalf of Company, and no approval or consent of any other person is necessary for Seller to enter or perform this Agreement.
3. Seller has no knowledge of any pending litigation, judgment, lien or proceeding relating to the Assets.

The representations and warranties section can include a number of guarantees, but should be minimized by the drafter to limit potential liability. Below is a list of the more common warranties made in this type of clause:

- Authority to conduct the transaction
- Existence of necessary licenses
- Intellectual property rights
- Statement of financial position
- Statement of tax liabilities
- Statement about any pending litigation
- Confirmation of adequate insurance

[4] The Disclaimer Clause

A disclaimer repudiates a warranty that may have existed or that a party might have claimed should have existed prior to the conclusion of the contract. Warranties may be disclaimed as well, such as a warranty of merchantability (that a good is fit for its ordinary purpose) or a warranty of fitness (that the goods are fit for the buyer's specific purpose, which he may not ultimately know). According to UCC § 2-316, the contract must explicitly state that the warranty of merchantability is being disclaimed if that is the intent (i.e., a general disclaimer will not eliminate the warranty of merchantability). An example of a disclaimer clause is found below.

Limited Warranty; Exclusion of Warranties.

1. Limited warranty. ABC warrants that it will perform any services required under this agreement in a commercially reasonable manner and will conform in material respects with the terms of this agreement.
2. Exclusion of warranties. All implied warranties and conditions of sale including, but not limited to, the implied warranties of merchantability and fitness for a particular purpose are expressly excluded from this agreement.

[5] The Indemnification Clause

An indemnification clause transfers liability affecting a party to a contract to the party that caused the damage. This clause would be appropriate in any contract in which a party is at risk of litigation as a result of the actions of the other party — for instance, a publisher who contracts with an author where the author might utilize copyrighted material in their publication, thus subjecting the publisher to liability. A sample clause is below.

Indemnification.

Consultant shall indemnify and defend Company from all damages, losses, costs, and expenses (including reasonable attorneys' fees and other costs of litigation) that arise out of or result from any claim that any work produced by Consultant pursuant to this Agreement infringes any copyright or other intellectual property right of any third party.

[6] The Merger Clause

The merger clause states that everything the parties intended to include in the text of the contract is in fact included. It attempts to limit representations and warranties to material stated in the contract by excluding any extraneous documents or discussions. It thereby strengthens the case against the introduction of parol evidence.

> *Entire Contract.*
>
> This contract, together with any attachments, exhibits or schedules herein referenced, constitutes the entire agreement of the parties concerning the sale of assets to the buyer. There are no oral representations, warranties, agreements, or promises pertaining to the sale of these assets that have not been incorporated into this contract.

[7] The Liquidated Damages Clause

It is often difficult for parties to predict or prove the amount of actual damages they would suffer in the event of a delay or other specific breaches of contract. A liquidated damages clause is meant to alleviate that by establishing a set amount of damages to be paid by either party in the event of minor breach. In many cases, the liquidated damages clause will reference the specific types of breach that will invoke liquidated damages. Other types of breach will be assessed by a judge or jury.

Liquidated damages may only be used if the injury that would be caused by the breach is difficult or impossible to estimate (e.g., release of a trade secret); the stipulated sum is a reasonable preliminary estimate of the probable loss (e.g., it was agreed upon by the parties in advance); and, the clause is not being used to punish the other party but rather to motivate them to avoid breach. Note that, unlike in some jurisdictions, U.S. courts will not sanction penalty clauses in contracts. When drafting a liquidated damages clause, the drafter must be very cautious in their word choice to prevent a court from interpreting the clause as a penalty clause. An example of a well-drafted liquidated damages clause is below.

> *Liquidated Damages.*
>
> If Builder fails to complete the agreed upon Project within the timeframe specified in Schedule A of the Agreement, Builder shall pay to Owner $2,000 for each calendar day that the delivery is delayed as liquidated damages. Parties agree that this is a reasonable estimate of the damages that Owner will accrue as a result of this delay and agree that this is not a penalty clause.

[8] The Term and Termination Clause

Every contract that you draft should have a clear start and end date, or a mechanism to determine its duration. The term and termination clause is where that information is usually found in a contract. This clause should answer the following questions:

- What is the duration of the contract?
- How can the contract be terminated?
- What happens after the contract is terminated?
- Is there a right to cure if there is breach?

How you draft this clause depends on the type of relationship you intend to form with the other party. Below are examples of three possible outcomes:

- Example of open-ended term: *This Agreement is effective when signed by both parties and remains in full force and effect until terminated by either party.*
- Example of definite term: *The term of this Lease begins on January 1, 2012 and, unless terminated sooner as provided below, the term expires on December 31, 2012.*
- Example with automatic renewals: Unless earlier terminated as provided below, this Agreement is effective as of the Effective Date and remains in force until twelve months from that date ("Initial Term"). After the Initial Term, this Agreement will be automatically renewed for successive one year periods unless either party notifies the other in writing on or before 30 days before the end of the then existing term.

[9] Severability/Saving Clause

In the event that a change in the law or a modification to the contract occurs where one or more clauses of the contract are deleted or found to be invalid, do you want to the contract to remain in force? The severability clause establishes what will happen in this instance. A sample clause is below.

> *Severability.*
>
> If any provision of this Agreement is deemed by a court having jurisdiction over this Agreement to be unenforceable to any extent, the rest of that provision and of this Agreement will remain in force to the fullest extent permitted by law.

[10] The Notice Clause

A notice clause is used to explain the logistics of providing notice to the other party. This may be notice that goods have been delivered, that a party has breached, or that a party plans to terminate the contract, among other things. The main points to address in this clause are the following:

- What constitutes proper notice — i.e., does notice have to be given by U.S. mail, FedEx, fax, email, or personal delivery?;
- How are days counted for purposes of notice — i.e., is notice deemed to be given on the day the buyer deposits a letter in the mail or when it is delivered into the seller's offices?;
- When is a party deemed to have received notice — i.e., is notice deemed received when it is placed in the mail or when it is actually received? What about electronic notices?

[11] Force Majeure Clause

The force majeure clause is intended to absolve a party of liability for non-performance when that non-performance is caused by circumstances beyond their control. It is a common misperception to assume that simply stating "force majeure" or "acts of God" will suffice to protect the parties in all cases. A wise contract drafter will spell-out clearly in this clause what constitutes force majeure and what the obligations of the parties are in such a case.

The two principal questions to address when drafting a force majeure clause are:

a. What events constitute force majeure?

b. What happens to the contract when one of these events occurs — is the contract suspended temporarily or terminated completely?

Consider the following sample clause.

Force Majeure.

Neither party is liable for failure to perform (except with respect to payment obligations) if that failure is directly caused by:

unavoidable casualty,

embargoes,

government orders, regulations, or directives,

acts of civil or military authorities,

acts by common carriers,

> emergency conditions (including weather conditions, terrorist events, and natural disasters), or
>
> any similar unforeseen event that renders performance commercially impracticable.
>
> In the event of one of these circumstances, the party injured by the other's inability to perform may elect one of the following remedies: (a) to terminate this Agreement in whole or in part; or (b) to suspend the Agreement, in whole or part, for the duration of the event impacting performance. The non-performing party will make good faith efforts to assist the injured party in all reasonable ways to minimize the impact of the injury, which may include locating and arranging substitute services if necessary.

[12] Waiver Clause

In some instances and for a variety of reasons, a party will accept slight deviations from the specific requirements of the contract. However, by accepting this deviation, the party may unwittingly be modifying the terms of the contract to allow such a deviation to occur legitimately under the agreement. To avoid this consequence, a waiver clause should be included in the contract. This will specify whether any deviation from the terms of the agreement, for any reason, signifies an acceptance of a contract modification.

> *Waivers.*
>
> Failure by either party to seek compensation for breach or insist upon strict performance of any covenant or condition of this Agreement does not prevent that party from seeking compensation or insisting upon strict performance for a future breach of that or any other provision of the Agreement.

[13] Counterparts

In the interest of efficiency and to facilitate contract transactions over long distances, contracts are often executed in counterparts. These are equal and equally valid versions of the same agreement. A counterparts clause defines how counterparts affect the validity of the terms and whether only one version controls in the event of a dispute over the meaning of a particular word or phrase.

In international contracts, foreign language versions of the same contract are common. In this case, a languages clause should be added to confirm the validity of versions in other languages and also to identify one language as the language of choice for interpretation. Bear in mind that English is not always the preferred language of interpretation in international agreements.

> *Counterparts.*
>
> This Sales Agreement may be executed in counterparts, each of which may be deemed an original but all of which constitute one and the same instrument.
>
> *Languages.*
>
> This Sales Agreement has been drafted contemporaneously in the English and Chinese languages. Both versions of the Sales Agreement are equally valid and enforceable. In the event of a dispute over the meaning of any provision of this Sales Agreement, the Chinese version shall be deemed the official version.

[14] Boilerplate Clauses

A boilerplate clause is a standard clause that a contract drafter inserts into similar contracts. These clauses are usually custom-designed by the drafter after significant research into the litigation in his or her jurisdiction surrounding the interpretation of that version of the clause. Most lawyers who draft contracts in the United States have a set of boilerplate clauses ready to be inserted into most contracts.

If you choose to keep a list of boilerplate clauses, be sure that you first assess their validity and any litigation associated with their use in other contracts. Also, always review them for appropriateness in the particular contract that you are drafting and be willing to adjust them based upon the individual circumstances of that contract.

[G] THE BACK OF THE CONTRACT

The back of the contract refers to the material following the body, such as the signature page and attachments. Little thought is paid to the importance of the back of the contract despite the fact that improper signature or misconstrued dates can invalidate or otherwise undermine the intent of the drafter.

[1] The Signature Page

The signature page begins with a concluding clause, transitioning from the body of the contract to the affirmation of the contracting parties. Some contracts that you come across may use language here such as: "In witness whereof, the parties hereto agree to execute and deliver and to be bound by the terms of this contract . . ." This legalese is unnecessarily wordy and confusing. Instead, consider using the following language:

- When a date is included in the introductory clause: *The parties hereby sign (or "are signing") this agreement on the date specified in the introductory clause.*
- When the specific type of contract should be emphasized: *The parties hereby sign (or "are signing") this agreement for the sale of goods on the date*

specified in the introductory clause.

- When the effective date depends on the signatories: *The parties hereby sign (or "are signing") this agreement, which becomes effective on the date associated with the last person to sign.*

Be careful with contracts that use the term "execute" on the signature page. To execute a contract in the United States, the parties must have the capacity to enter into the agreement and they must comply with any required formalities of that execution. This may mean that the signatory must assert, via the representations clause, that he or she has the authority to bind the party on whose behalf they are signing. A signature is not the equivalent of an execution.

The parties hereby sign this agreement, which becomes effective on the date associated with the last person to sign.

	Simpson Electronics, LLC
Date: ________________	By: ______________ Homer Simpson Chief Executive Officer
	Burns Industries, Inc.
Date: ________________	By: ______________ Montgomery Burns Contracting Officer

[2] Attachments, Exhibits, and Schedules

If you intend to include additional documentation with the contract, such as production schedules or financing terms, you may wish to do so as supplements to the body of the contract. If you do, you should refer to them throughout the contract by their appropriate name (e.g., "found in Attachment A"). These additional items, once referenced in the body of the contract, become a binding part of the contract.

- Attachments: These are materials that are attached directly to the contract and may include, among other things, financing provisions, integrated letters of intent, and other reference materials.
- Exhibits: These are materials extraneous to the contract that are incorporated by reference. Exhibits usually consist of examples or samples associated with the terms of the contract, or may reference a document that has not yet been finalized. They are referenced directly in the agreement but are not attached to it.
- Schedules: These are common in construction contracts and other agreements that provide for specific dates of performance that would be too lengthy to include in the body of the contract. They are attached to the contract and referenced in the body of the contract.

[H] DRAFTING POINTERS

[1] Numbers and Currency

Time of day, currency, and numbers in general can create great confusion and lead to significant liability for a client in the event of a mistake in drafting. Working in international contracts complicates this issue further as different designations are used for currency and even to establish time.

[2] Tips on Drafting Time of Day

- Always note the time zone. A contract calling for delivery by 5:00pm in New York by a Chinese company may lead to a 12-hour delay if no time zone is specified.
- Consider daylight savings time. Most states in the United States and most countries in Europe observe daylight savings time (also known as "summer time"). This means that clocks are turned back one hour in autumn and turned ahead one hour in spring to extend daylight throughout the year. Note that Arizona does not follow daylight savings time.
- The proper designations for time are A.M. (ante-meridiem) and P.M. (post-meridiem); however, there is often confusion about when to use each. A.M. is used for all times beginning with 12:00 midnight and running through 11:59 in the morning. At noon or midday, P.M. is used to designate time and continues to do so through 11:59 in the evening.

[3] Tips on Drafting Currency

- Currency should always be drafted with a designation for the type of currency. These designations can be either a currency symbol (e.g., $, ¥, £) or a three letter designation derived from the international standard for currency designations (e.g., EUR, JPY). Currency designations can be found via ISO Standard 4217 here: http://www.xe.com/iso4217.php.
- Note that the $ is generally used for dollar and peso denominations:
    - COL$1,000 = one thousand Colombian pesos
    - A$1,000 = one thousand Australian dollars
    - CLP$1,000 = one thousand Chilean pesos
- Other currencies utilize the ISO 4217 3-letter convention or symbol:
    - EUR 1,000 or €1,000 = 1,000 Euros
    - JPY 1,000 or ¥1,000 = 1,000 Yen
- When working with large amounts of currency, be sure to use the proper numerals:
    - $1,000 = one thousand dollars

  - $1,000,000 = one million dollars
  - $1,000,000,000 = one billion dollars
- Decimals
  - Do not use numerals after decimal points unless referencing cents: i.e., $5.36 is acceptable; $5.00 is not acceptable

[4] Drafting Numbers

- Conventionally, contracts contained both numerals and written-out numbers (e.g., $5,000 (five thousand dollars)). This was intended to prevent any potential error in drafting the amount. However, the practice is cumbersome and not necessary in modern contracts. When drafting a contract, utilize the numeral rather than the numeric words when designating currency. Otherwise, follow the rule below.
- In general, numbers should be written-out if they are ten or smaller. Numerals should be used for any number larger than ten.
  - Example: I have seven children. Each of my children has to read 15 books this year.
  - Example: On the first of the month, we will celebrate my birthday. We plan to visit a restaurant on 13th street for the celebration.
- However, be consistent with the use of numerals and words if the passage is mixed. Generally, use of numerals is preferred.
  - Example: There were 5 cats and 25 dogs.
- Percentages should be in numeral form.
  - Example: The bank is charging 5% interest on this loan.
- If two numbers are next to each other, spell one of them out.
  - Example: The agents seized the drugs, weapons, and fifty $100 bills from the stash house.
- Always spell-out numbers that start sentences.
  - Example: Fifty-seven people attended the trial.

[I] WHY DO WE WANT A WRITTEN CONTRACT IN THE FIRST PLACE?

Oral contracts in the United States are generally valid. In fact, they happen all the time. Each time a customer enters a restaurant and orders food from the menu, they are entering into an oral agreement with that establishment to pay for that food once received. Yet oral contracts are particularly susceptible to fraud as well, as in the case where a car dealer promises you a price on a certain vehicle and then, when it comes time to make payment, the price has increased.

Certain types of oral contracts, particularly those subject to a high possibility of fraud, must be in writing if they are to be enforced by a court of law. The statute of frauds, which was originally established in England in 1677 and has since made its way into law in the United States, requires the following types of agreements, among others, to be written before a court will enforce them:

- Sales of real property (e.g., land, houses, apartments)
- Sales of goods where the goods are valued at more than $500
- Contracts that cannot be performed in less than one year (e.g., an agreement to purchase stock that can only be executed after 12 months)
- Prenuptial agreements (in anticipation of marriage)

Agreements of this type that are completed verbally are valid; however, in the event of a dispute, the defending party may invoke the statute of frauds to prevent a court from enforcing the agreement. This is why it is always better to have a written contract, even for many minor transactions.

There can be significant consequences for entering into an oral agreement rather than a written agreement. Consider the 1987 case of *Pennzoil v. Texaco.*[33] In this famous case, Pennzoil entered into negotiations to merge with another company, Getty. The agreement was drafted and agreed to orally by senior officials from both companies; however, the written agreement stated that it was subject to the approval of the board of directors from each company, which it had not yet received. Prior to the conclusion of the written agreement, another company, Texaco, lured Getty away with a better merger offer. Pennzoil sued Texaco for tortious interference.

Whether an oral agreement or, as in this case, an oral agreement supported by an unsigned written agreement, binds the parties is a question of fact that a judge or jury will determine in the event of a dispute. In this case, the jury found that there was sufficient evidence to prove that Pennzoil and Getty intended to be bound by the terms of the agreement, thus forming a valid and binding contract. Accordingly, Texaco was found liable for tortious interference and was subjected to damages of $11 billion, including a $3 billion punitive damage finding. The parties later settled the case for $3 billion after Texaco filed for bankruptcy.

Note that oral agreements that fall within the statute of frauds subject areas may still be enforced if they have been fully (common law) or partially (UCC) executed. For instance, an oral agreement for the sale of goods valued at more than $500, which would normally be unenforceable due to the statute of frauds, would be perfectly valid and enforced if the parties already concluded the transaction and a dispute occurred after the execution.

But that is not the only risk you can face when you fail to memorialize an agreement in writing. You also face the difficulty, in the event of a dispute, of proving the terms of the agreement. In general, assuming you are not facing a statute of frauds defense, a court will rely on witness testimony, related writings between the parties (e.g.,

---

[33] *Texaco, Inc. v. Pennzoil Co.*, 729 S.W.2d 768 (Tex. App. 1987).

letters of intent), and evidence of prior dealings between the parties. None of these unequivocally represent that intent of the parties, so the result is likely unbalanced and not necessarily what you, or your client, expected.

Similar to a written contract, oral agreements require the existence of basic elements of contract formation, such as a valid offer and acceptance, inclusion of the price, quantity, and description terms, and the legal capacity of the parties to enter into an agreement. The greater the complexity of the terms and language of the oral agreement, the more difficult it becomes to demonstrate the satisfaction of these essential requirements of a valid contract.

In the event of a dispute over the existence or terms of an executed oral contract, courts will often look to credibility of witness testimony, any prior course of conduct, whether the parties commenced performance of the contract, or whether payment was transferred from the buyer to the seller. If the parties have made an oral agreement but not yet begun to carry out the terms of the agreement, a court may find the oral agreement unenforceable without proof of the terms memorialized in a written document. For example, in a case disputing whether a corporation had orally agreed to sell shares of its corporate stock, a court found that "[t]he alleged oral contract is too vague and uncertain to be enforced," *Marshall v. W.E. Marshall Co.*, and "[t]hese deficiencies were not cured by performance of the plaintiff, because the agreement relied upon was so vague, indefinite and uncertain as to make it impossible for courts to determine what, if anything, was agreed upon, therefore rendering it impossible to determine whether there had been performance."[34]

Or, consider the case of *Illinois Light Co. v. Consolidation Coal Co.*, which involved an oral agreement for the provision of coal at a specific price over a two-year period.[35] After the oral agreement had been concluded, the parties exchanged a number of draft contracts and emails discussing the terms of the arrangement, and the Illinois Light Company began shipping coal at the price specified in the draft contracts. However, they discontinued their shipments and Consolidation Coal thereafter filed suit for breach of contract. In this case, the court found that since no written agreement was ever reached, and since this contract involved the sale of goods valued at over $500, the court could not enforce it as a contract.

These cases show us that parties frequently enter into oral agreements, either as a more convenient mechanism to conduct business or as a preliminary measure while hammering-out the final details of a written agreement. But they also show us that the enforceability of an oral contract is far weaker than that of a written contract. To protect your clients, it is advisable to always draft, negotiate and sign (i.e., execute) a written contract to prevent unnecessary complications in contract enforcement in the event of a dispute.

---

[34] 376 S.E.2d 393, 396 (Ga. App. 1988) (internal quotation and citation omitted).

[35] 349 F.3d 488, 492 (7th Cir. 2003).

[J] PROMISSORY ESTOPPEL AND RELIANCE

Promissory estoppel is an equitable doctrine that prevents a person who makes a promise from rescinding that promise after someone has expectedly relied upon that promise to their detriment. It is frequently used in oral contract cases to prove the existence of an agreement despite lack of evidence of consideration or some other contractual formality that would otherwise prevent the enforcement of the agreement.

The Restatement of Contracts, a recognized source of legal interpretation, defines promissory estoppel as follows:

> "When a promisee foreseeably relies to his detriment on the promisor's promise, even in the absence of an enforceable contract, the doctrine of promissory estoppel may be invoked to make such promise binding in order to prevent injustice. The remedy in such cases is based on the extent of the promisee's reliance, not his expectation. The Restatement, Second, eliminated the requirement from the Restatement, First, that the detriment be 'substantial.' "[36]

Among other examples, the Restatement discusses the use of this doctrine in cases in which land is promised orally, the recipient takes possession and makes improvements, and then the land is reclaimed by the original owner for lack of a valid contract; donations to philanthropic organizations (i.e., charities), which lack consideration; and letters of intent in which one party believes the transaction will go forward but the other abandons the negotiations.

[K] PAROL EVIDENCE

Even after a contract has been properly written and signed by the parties, disputes over what was intended with the contract can arise. In some cases, a party to a written contract may attempt to provide evidence of the parties' intent through the introduction of prior oral evidence, such as conversation between the parties during contract negotiations. In general, this type of evidence is impermissible to prove the intent of the parties.

The parol (i.e., oral) evidence rule exists to prevent parties from introducing evidence of prior intent once a contract has been fully and finally reduced to writing. If the party defending against the introduction of such evidence proves that a written contract is final or fully integrated, a court will not allow the other party to enter evidence as to prior discussions. The assumption is that once the parties have documented their intent in a final contract, there is no reason to allow conflicting evidence of prior discussions to be introduced to challenge that final contract.

If the prior evidence would be used to rectify an ambiguity in the contract, to correct a mistake, or to prove fraud, a court may admit it. Also, if the court finds that the contract is not in fact final and that everything the parties intended is not found in the "four corners" of the contract, the court may admit the prior evidence.

---

[36] Restatement (2d) of Contracts § 90 (1).

To avoid the possibility of prior oral discussions being allowed to challenge the intent of the parties in a contract, lawyers developed the merger clause. The merger clause, which is discussed below, allows each party to attest to the fact that everything they intended to include in the contract is in fact within the contract as it is written. This avoids a challenge to the finality of the contract.

Goals of contract drafting:

- Draft for the client, not for the opposing counsel or judge.
- Make the document as readable and clear as possible.
- Pay close attention to the language used, especially if it is from opposing counsel or boilerplate.

Chapter 7

ACADEMIC LEGAL WRITING

[A] INTRODUCTION

Successful advocates for their clients often become successful advocates for issues as well. Through their training and practice, legal practitioners often develop skills in research and persuasive writing. This leads some of them to research and write academic articles in law journals, policy journals, and other academic forums. This section of the text will address the different style of legal writing used to produce academic pieces and how to go about finding a publisher once you complete an article.

Topics Covered in This Chapter:

- Finding and Selecting a Topic
- Developing a Research Question
- Integrating Research into an Outline
- Keeping the Reader Engaged and Interested
- Balancing Research with Opinion
- Polishing the Document
- Publishing the Article

[B] TYPES OF ACADEMIC LEGAL WRITING

Academic legal writing is quite distinct from other forms of legal writing. The goal of an academic piece is to identify and analyze a relevant and important issue in law or policy and to do so in a way that is both convincing and interesting. An academic piece may ultimately end up being published in a law or policy journal; it may form part of a book on a particular subject; or it may serve as a piece of the policy analysis process for the issue itself.

What makes academic legal writing distinct from other legal documents is the need for well-supported and carefully drafted statements. Unlike in a legal memorandum, where you are presenting the state of a particular legal issue, academic writing attempts to profoundly analyze an issue in a new light using existing sources as a foundation. It requires the writer to be acutely aware of the current and past state of affairs, and attuned to how and why the issue should be addressed in a new way in the future.

[1] Case Analyses

In the case of a review and analysis of a recent Supreme Court decision, for instance, a writer might analyze why the Court relied on certain precedents as opposed to others, the procedural history of the case, and the key facts that set that case apart from similar cases and led it to the Supreme Court. But, unlike other legal writing, the academic writer will go further and explain how this decision will change the face of the law in this area, how this case is indicative of a new trend within the Court, or how this decision will likely prompt a push for new legislation from Congress. An academic analysis of a case requires the writer to think ahead and to address issues that others have likely addressed but in a novel and useful way.

Some examples of topics in this area might be:

- The Impact of the X Decision on International Human Rights Law
- Comparing "Boxtop" Licenses across Circuit Courts
- The Famous "Footnote 4" in the *Carolene Products* Case

[2] Issue Papers

If the article is intended instead to analyze a particular issue, the key for an academic legal writer is to take a new approach to an old (or new) problem. This could mean approaching an issue in tort law from a criminal law perspective, or addressing a domestic law from an international law focus. It could be as simple as asking a question that no one has yet asked, or as complex as applying a grand theory from another discipline to a mundane legal issue to inject fresh insights. An issue paper is often the most interesting to write because it allows vast creativity in the approach. But the development of such an article follows the same steps as a case analysis.

Some examples of topics in this area might be:

- A Legal Analysis of the "Rare Earths" Dispute between the U.S. and China
- Rule of Law and the Weakening State in Egypt
- Reforming the WTO to Address the Needs of Developing Countries

[C] STAGES OF ACADEMIC LEGAL WRITING

The structure of academic writing is methodical. There are certain steps that must be completed in order to produce a complete, coherent, and publication-worthy piece. These stages of the writing process ensure that the right amount of legal research has been completed, that assertions are properly supported, and that the conclusion logically follows from the argument.

Yet, this process is not intended to be rigid or inflexible. Most of the legal professionals that engage in academic writing have other jobs, so their time is limited and valuable. Additionally, ideas come at different moments in the process and you aren't expected to ignore those ideas simply because you haven't reached that stage in the writing process yet. It is good to get your ideas out when they are fresh in your mind so that you don't lose them.

The key stages of the academic legal writing process are as follows:

1. Formulate a research topic
2. Turn your research topic into a research question
3. Outline your manuscript
4. Develop and execute a research plan
5. Analyze material with original writing
6. Connect thoughts with transitions and headings
7. Validate Authorities
8. Wrap-up the Article

Next, let's examine each of these stages in a succinct and clear manner.

[1] Stage 1: Formulating a Research Topic

The first stage in academic legal writing is often the most exciting. For most academic legal writers, this is also the easiest stage since every good piece of legal writing begins with an idea that we already have in our heads. Others, who may be writing out of some obligation (e.g., a school assignment or writing sample for a job), may find this stage more difficult.

Yet, no matter why we are writing, it is important to realize that not every topic is viable. Some topics may have already been over-analyzed and, unless our approach adds something entirely new and fresh to the issue, another piece would hardly get noticed. Some topics are outdated and archaic. Articles on these issues, while interesting to historians and perhaps academics who specialize in these areas, a broader audience may find such work less enticing. So, before beginning any work on an idea that you have, answer the following questions:

- Why is your topic important? Consider the value of the research you intend to perform and whether it will benefit anyone other than you.
- Who is going to read my article? Knowing your audience is critical in selecting a topic. If you will write for a bar journal, for instance, keep your topic practical and concise. If you are writing a chapter for a book, know the theme of the book and to whom it is marketed to.
- How broad should my topic be? Most academic papers are narrowly focused, addressing a single key issue in great detail. However, some survey pieces are written to introduce a subject to readers who may be unfamiliar with it. Decide this as early as possible.
- Is this a legal argument or a law/policy argument? Legal writing is flexible enough to allow you to draft an analysis of a case or complicated legal issue relying mostly on jurisprudence as your sources, or to draft a policy-oriented

article that intersperses jurisprudence and other scholarly work to produce a piece that will be more widely read outside the legal community.

[a] *Finding a Topic*

Now that you have a structure in mind for your topic, how do you actually nail down an idea and identify what your topic will be? First, you must find a source of inspiration. No matter how intelligent or creative you are, most great topics begin in other sources. Depending on the approach that you plan to take — legal argument or law/ policy analysis — you can turn to a set of sources that both inspire and enlighten:

Legal Argument Topic Ideas

- Recent Supreme Court or federal court cases (consider reviewing these on www.oyez.com)
- An important case in an area of your interest (use Google Scholar or LexisNexis to search for cases in a particular area of law)
- New federal or state statute that could have important consequences (consider reviewing these on www.thomas.gov)
- New rules and regulations proposed or implemented by federal agencies (consider reviewing these on www.regulations.gov)

Law/Policy Analysis Topic Ideas

- Law review articles that raise interesting points of law (think about what the article overlooked or what you would approach differently)
- News articles (some good sources include the Economist, Washington Post, New York Times, Financial Times, and the Wall Street Journal)
- International news (consider foreign news sources in the part of the world where you want to focus your topic)
- Conferences and speeches (attend events, such as bar association meetings, and take notes on presentations, which often have excellent ideas but insufficient academic research behind them)

Once you have a good topic in mind, you've identified your audience of readers, and you've determined that the topic is important enough to write about, answer the following questions:

I. Is it novel? In other words, has your topic already been extensively discussed by other authors.

   a. Examples:

      - Not Novel: Evaluation of trade promotion authority for U.S. presidents.
      - Novel: How TPA has effectively undermined the power of Congress to check the Executive in its arbitrary trade actions.

- Not Novel: *Brown vs. Board of Education* set in motion the foundation for affirmative action programs in Universities today.
- Novel: *Brown v. Board of Education* can serve as the basis for challenging school policies that restrict illegal immigrant children from enrolling in school.

II. Does it raise issues that would be interesting to a broad audience?

a. Narrow: Hormone growth treatments can negatively affect the development of cattle in the Western U.S. (better for a science journal).

b. Better: Hormone growth treatments given to cattle in the Western U.S. can lead to unwanted chemicals passed into dairy products.

c. Best: Cattle that are given hormone growth treatments may produce dairy products that harm consumers.

III. Is it an issue that reasonable conclusions can be drawn about?

a. Difficult: The U.S. President's foreign policy power is too broad and should be limited.

b. Better: The Sixth Circuit ruling in the *Bakke* case may affect admissions policies in U.S. universities.

IV. Is it a purely political/ opinionated issue rather than a legal issue?

a. Political: Bill Clinton acted immorally and was a bad leader as a result.

b. Better: Should the personal life of a President be called into question when making foreign policy decisions?

c. Best: Presidents should be immune from civil prosecution while in office because it impedes their ability to conduct effective foreign policy.

V. Is it too complicated?

a. Complicated: The tax code should be rewritten to focus on poverty reduction rather than federal revenue.

b. Less complicated: The mortgage interest deduction in the U.S. tax code should be limited to families making less than $200,000 per year.

[2] Stage 2: Turning Your Research Topic into a Research Question

Now that you have a great topic and you know that it is going to lead to an important and useful analysis of a novel issue, it is time to convert that topic into a research question. Much like the process in turning your client's facts into a legal question when you are drafting a legal memorandum, this process is a matter of formulating the topic so that your research stays focused and narrow enough to be answered in a 30 or 40 page article. Your goals in this process are to convert your topic into a question that you can answer through good research, and to draft a these statement that explains, in a few lines, why the topic is important and how you will address it.

Turning the Topic into a Question

When you convert your topic into a question, you can more easily identify sources that answer that question. This helps you stay focused and avoid straying into tangentially-related topics. Consider the following examples:

- Topic: The impact of migrant remittances in Guatemala.
    - Research question: Do remittances from Guatemalan migrants contribute to economic development and stability?
- Topic: The failed use of the Commerce Clause in the Affordable Health Care Act decision.
    - Research question: Has the U.S. Supreme Court effectively constrained Congress's ability to use the Commerce Clause as a result of the Affordable Health Care Act decision?

Drafting a Thesis Statement

Your thesis statement is an expansion of your research question. This is your attempt to encapsulate all of the questions you asked in stage 1 into a single paragraph. Your goal is to effectively convey your topic, explain why it matters, discuss why it has not yet been properly address, and state how you will address it. Accordingly, your thesis statement should be structured as follows:

Sentence 1: State your research question.

Example: Do remittances from Guatemalan migrants contribute to economic development and stability?

Sentences 2-3: State why this question matters.

Example: The most productive individuals in the country have fled to the United States to seek work; however, they send home remittances to sustain their families and their communities. These remittances are not regulated or taxed by the Guatemalan government.

Sentences 3-4: State why existing research fails to address it.

Example: Existing research has examined the impact of remittances on local communities, but not the impact of remittances on the broader national economy.

Final Sentence: State how you will address it.

Example: In this article, I will endeavor to analyze national-level data on remittances and economic growth in order to uncover the real effects of this lost productive labor combined with remittances on the national economy in Guatemala.

[3] Stage 3: Outline Your Manuscript

Perhaps one of the most important parts of drafting an article, an outline is a methodical organization of your arguments. Once your outline is properly drafted, and your research is done, your paper will fill in the gaps like puzzle pieces.

Do not skip this stage, even if you choose not to utilize the outline once you begin drafting. Your initial outline does not need a particular format of organization — that comes later. At this stage, focus on getting the ideas out on paper so that you can see clearly the scope of the project.

An outline is useful for keeping you on track in terms of what you will be writing and how soon it will be complete. It is also useful to help you jump around to different sections without fear of losing the main idea. As long as the sections you jump to are within the outline, then you can rest assured that your research and writing will not be in vain. The outline offers you a macro perspective on the paper. You can see all of the areas that your paper will cover before you've begun drafting. Be sure you haven't left anything out and that your argument makes sense.

Keep in mind that outlining is a living process. Like a draft, your first outline will not be your last. Don't hesitate to remove sections of the outline that you feel are redundant or outside the scope of your research; and certainly add in ideas that you come across in your research and find essential to the context of your discussion.

Break your research question down into its component parts. Think about the importance of each element and how you might address it. Then think about how you will unify those elements throughout your article.

Your outline should consist of the following sections:

- Introduction/ Topic Overview
- Background on the Topic
- Issue Component 1
- Issue Component 2
- Issue Component 3
- Issue Unification
- Conclusion

Note that the number of issue components depends on your research question. Also, you may have sub-components within a single component that need to be addressed. For instance, if your research question asks whether the free trade agreement between the U.S. and Colombia is promoting economic development and fair trade between those countries, you might structure your outline like this:

- Introduction to the Free Trade Agreement between these two countries; statement of thesis
- Background on fair trade and economic development

- Component 1: Examination of trade policy in the hemisphere
    - Latin American trade policy analysis
    - Colombia's trade policy analysis
    - Previous attempts to build free trade relationships
- Component 2: Using bilateral trade to promote policy goals
- Component 3: Analysis of the U.S.-Colombia Agreement
    - Elements of the Agreement
    - Data on the impact of the Agreement
- Conclusions and recommendations

[4] Stage 4: Develop and Execute a Research Plan

Now that your outline is drafted, you have a roadmap to work with in carrying-out your research. So — where do you begin?

Get to Know Your Issue

The first step in any effective research strategy is topic familiarization. Using secondary sources, such as law review articles, news pieces, books, and online materials, read everything that you can about your topic. You may already know a great deal about the topic, which is terrific. But, there may be gaps in your knowledge, and, if you are to establish or maintain a good reputation as a published author, you must be considered a competent authority in the subject. Read everything you can about the topic, attend lectures and conferences about the topic, and make sure that you can speak fluently about it without any hesitation.

Use Foundational Sources for Background

The second step is to present the background on the issue to your reader. This step serves two purposes. It helps your reader better understand the topic and why it matters, and it helps you to further expand and communicate your knowledge of the topic to your audience. Don't hesitate to provide more extensive background here than you might ordinarily write. You can reduce this later once you have discerned exactly what is crucial to know and what can be cut out.

Step into Your Headings

Using your outline, select one of the components where you want to begin your research. Use that component heading to guide your searches, starting with online sources such as Google Scholar, and working your way toward specific sources found on LexisNexis, Westlaw, and JSTOR, among others.

Every time you come upon a source, whether it is a news piece, journal article, book, or case, review it quickly to assess whether it fits into your theme. If it does, review the piece and write down the key points within that section of your article, using the outline to set out the headings. Be sure to note the citation information for the source and include that as a footnote to whatever text you add to your article. This will be crucial later when you need to move material around and dig deeper in certain segments of your article.

Repeat this process for each component, breaking-out additional sub-components if necessary. You should have at least ten useful and unique sources within each component before you begin the next stage.

[5] Stage 5: Analyze Material with Original Writing

As you begin to see your article unfold before your eyes and each component is filling up with useful and interesting material, you need to begin thinking about critical writing. At this stage, you have likely come upon numerous sources that agree with your ideas and you may have used these sources to shape and give support to your arguments. However, it is essential that you include sources that take a different approach as well and that you read all sources in a critical light.

An academic legal writer is an astute analyst, finding gaps in arguments and exposing weaknesses in analyses. One of the most important tools that you have developed as a legal professional is the ability to critically analyze. Apply that skill here by taking original text or summaries that you have prepared of your sources and present them to the reader with a dose of your critical analysis. For instance:

> In Tobin's seminal work, *Jerry the Rockstar*, he argues that Jerry Brown was born to play the guitar. [citation] However, Jerry Brown was actually trained as a concert pianist and only took up his interest in the guitar when he was in his mid-thirties.

In this fictitious example, the author is highlighting one of his sources and explaining how it is misleading. The ability to critically assess sources sets apart mediocre writers and great writers. Keep this in mind as you insert information from your research.

[6] Stage 6: Connect Thoughts with Transitions and Headings

At this stage, you should have a large portion of your research complete. Each component should be overflowing with useful material and you should have numerous sources scattered throughout the article. However, what you probably do not yet have is a thread throughout the article that connects all of the ideas you have collected.

So, your next job is to link these ideas together. Select a component and begin by reviewing the material that you have collected there. With that material in mind, draft a short introductory paragraph for that section. Then, reorganize the material so that you have background readings for that component first, followed by supporting arguments and analysis, and finally contrary arguments and analysis.

Apply transitions between paragraphs to connect the thoughts between each one. Transitions allow the reader to flow through your document without stopping suddenly to shift gears. They maintain a single idea and keep the reader focused on that idea throughout the section.

Your transitions should stem from the single idea you are trying to convey in that component or sub-component. Use that heading or opening paragraph to guide you as you insert transitions throughout the section. And keep in mind that if you cannot identify an appropriate transition that links the two paragraphs together, either they are disorganized or you are missing a crucial piece of your analysis.

There are generally two types of transitions that you can use to connect paragraphs together. The first is a simple transition and it uses a single word to indicate to the reader that the same idea is continuing.

> Example: One of the defenses to the enforcement of an oral contract is known as the statute of frauds. This statute was first used in England four hundred years ago. It was meant to reduce the likelihood of fraud in contract claims. The United States adopted the principles of the statute of frauds in their common law system.
>
> However, the statute of frauds in the United States is unique in that it specifies exactly which types of claims qualify for protection from enforcement.

Note that in this case, the word "however" was used to indicate that the second paragraph will continue the same analysis as the first paragraph, but that it will introduce something new as well. This type of transition is quite frequently used to link paragraphs in books and articles. But, there are more advanced transitions that can also be used.

An advanced transition takes a thought or idea from the first paragraph and reiterates it in a different form in the second paragraph. This makes for a seamless link between the two ideas and allows the reader to continue along the same thread uninterrupted.

> Example: One of the defenses to the enforcement of an oral contract is known as the statute of frauds. This statute was first used in England four hundred years ago. It was meant to reduce the likelihood of fraud in contract claims. The United States adopted the principles of the statute of frauds in their common law system.
>
> These principles were refined and narrowed by the time the United States adopted the statute of frauds.

Note that in this case the phrase "these principles" was used to link together the basic idea of the first paragraph with the idea of the second paragraph. There was no need to use a transition word here since that phrase successfully glued the two paragraphs together. Advanced transitions provide for smoother writing and smoother reading.

Be sure to conclude each component section with a mini-conclusion. A one-paragraph summary of what you covered in that section is an effective way to encapsulate the main points and give the reader a succinct thought to take with them into the next section of the article.

[7] Stage 7: Validating Authorities

Once you have successfully linked-up your paragraphs in each component and sub-component and provided introductions and conclusions to each section, you are ready to begin the validation process. Do not skip this stage as it is necessary to give you confidence that your sources are reputable and accurate and that your assertions are properly supported.

Validation of Authorities

The last thing that you want after spending weeks researching and writing your article is for a critic to notice a case that is no longer good law that you relied on to make a central point, or even an article by an author that is considered far afield of mainstream thought on the idea. So, before you face those critics, validate your sources.

For cases, validation is a matter of using the Shepard's or Keycite tools in LexisNexis or Westlaw, respectively. Any negative treatment of your case should be carefully reviewed and assessed to ensure that your authority is still good law. If you do not have access to these databases, you can search for articles about your cases on Google Scholar and determine whether the cases have been positively received.

For articles, learn about your authors. If they are professors, review their university web site and examine their areas of expertise. If they are practitioners, do the same on their firm or organization's web page, if available. Did they write their article as a side project or is it actually an area in which they are considered to be experts? If they are not experts, consider looking to other sources to make sure you include reference to the key authors in the field.

[8] Stage 8: Wrapping-Up the Article

And now for the moment you've been waiting for — finishing the article. The hard work is over. This final stage asks you to put the finishing touches on the article and to prepare it for publication. In this stage, use the following checklist to ensure that you have completed everything you need to in order to have the piece ready to go final:

- Revise the introductory paragraph to match the final theme of the article.
- Ensure that you have drafted a conclusion section that includes a summary of the points made in each component along with a list of recommendations for further action or study.
- Make sure that all citations are properly formatted in BlueBook or APA style, depending on where you submit the piece for publication.
- Apply a single font style and size throughout the document.
- Add page numbers.
- Add a cover page with the title and your name and affiliation (firm or university).

- Edit for spelling, grammar, punctuation, and style mistakes.

As a final tip, I recommend that you send the piece to at least three colleagues, preferably in a mix of areas of expertise, and ask them to provide you with their comments on the article before you submit it for publication. The feedback that you receive from these colleagues will likely be positive, but it may also help you better understand how the article will be received by readers and what questions those readers may have after having read your article. You have a chance to address some of these before you submit it to be published.

No article is ever truly finished. Rather, it goes to publication with questions remaining in your mind. Don't be afraid of this. Any expert knows that a thorough analysis of a single research question will never conclusively answer that question. Use this to your advantage. Once you finally conclude this piece and send it off to be considered for publication, write down some of those outstanding questions you have in your mind. Use those to begin formulating your next research questions. You will find that once you begin the process of academic writing and publication, you will never want to stop.

Chapter 8

LEGAL CITATION

[A] INTRODUCTION

It is fair to say that legal citation is one of the most confusing practices of American legal practice. Knowing when to cite, how to cite, and the importance of citation is a skill often outside the training of even the most experienced non-U.S. legal practitioners. This section will explain the rationale of effective legal citation and some tips on formatting sources properly.

Topics Covered in This Chapter:

- Why Citing Properly is Required
- How Citations Differ Depending on Type of Document
- A Short Review of the BlueBook
- Saving Time Using Technology to Cite

[B] THE IMPORTANCE OF LEGAL CITATION

Though it may seem mundane, proper legal citation is a reflection of quality legal writing. Whether you are preparing a brief for court, writing an article for a law review, or publishing a treatise, legal citation should be on your agenda.

Citation refers to the identification of external documents or other sources that you either relied upon for your analysis or that you paraphrased or quoted from. Citation is an accepted practice in U.S. legal writing. It is often expected in U.S. legal documents. Citation is required if in any way referencing a source other than your own opinion.

Proper citation serves a number of functions. First, it supports the assertions the author is making. This may be as simple as referencing the case or book from which a quote that you used came, or it may be a series of sources that you analyzed in order to construct your statement in the main text. Second, it provides the reader with access to further reading on points that may be of interest to them but that were not expounded upon in the main text. And third, it provides credit to the authors of the sources that you used in your research.

Citation in U.S. legal writing follows the BlueBook style manual, available online and in U.S. bookstores. The BlueBook is a compendium of legal citation published by the editors of the Harvard, Columbia, Yale, and University of Pennsylvania Law

Reviews. It was first published in 1926 and took the name "The BlueBook" in 1981. It is the principal source used by legal professionals in the United States for citation in all legal documents. Unless you are submitting a document to a court that has unique rules, the BlueBook is the recommended style for all of your legal writing citation.

The BlueBook contains style requirements for most types of legal documents, including cases, statutes, law journal articles, web sites, and foreign courts. However, there are some documents that you may encounter, especially from non-U.S. sources, that the BlueBook does not reference. Accordingly, if you cannot find your specific source in the BlueBook, attempt to find a similar source and follow that format for your source.

Below you will find a list of the most commonly cited documents in legal writing with an explanation next to each of what each element in the citation means. Note that citation is highly precise, so commas and spaces matter if you plan to cite properly.

<u>Citing a case from a U.S. court</u>

Vidal v. Gonzales, 491 F.3d 250, 254 (5th Cir. 2007).

- Only the party's last names are used. Eliminate additional text (e.g., Inc., LLC, bros.).
- Always underline or italicize the party names (be consistent in all citations).
- 491 refers to the volume of the reporter in which this case is found.
- F.3d (Federal Third) refers to the name of the reporter in which this case is found.
- 250 refers to the first page on which this case appears in that reporter.
- 254 refers to the specific page on which the reader can find the referenced text.
- 5th Cir. (Fifth Circuit) refers to the specific court in which the case was heard.
- 2007 refers to the year of the decision.

Vidal v. Gonzalez, No. 56-245, slip op. at 14 (W.D. Cal. Jan. 26, 2007).

- This is a *slip opinion*, which means a case that has not yet been officially published.
- This type of case can still be used as precedent.

Vidal v. Gonzalez, No. 56-245, 2007 WL56172, at *14 (W.D. Cal. Jan. 26, 2007).

- This is a case either too new to be reported or unpublished, but available online using either Westlaw or LexisNexis.

<u>Citing a U.S. Statute</u>

Department of Transportation Act, Pub. L. No. 89-670, § 9, 80 Stat. 931, 944-47 (1966).

- Always identify the common name of the statute (if there is one) first.

- Include both the Public Law Number and the statutory reference, where possible.
- The date used is the date the statute was enacted.

19 U.S.C. § 1508 (2007).

- If citing to a section of the U.S. Code (U.S.C.), refer to it this way.
- 19 refers to the Title/Volume of the U.S. Code in which this section appears.
- Always use the § symbol to refer to the section in legal writing.
- 1508 refers to the section of this title of the code.
- The year used is the most recent edition (unless you intend to reference an older version).

7 C.F.R. § 1331 (2000).

- If citing to the Code of Federal Regulations (C.F.R.), refer to in this format.
- 7 refers to the volume of the code in which the section appears.
- 1331 refers to the section or Part of the C.F.R. being referenced
- The year used is the most recent edition (unless you intend to reference an older version).

Citing Foreign Legal Sources in a U.S. Legal Document

Statutes

The Labor Procedure Act (R.C.L. 1990, 922) (Spain).

- R.C.L. refers to the *Repertorio Aranzadi Cronológico de Legislación* (note that every country has different names for statutes).

Cases

Weed v. Powell, [1978] S.C.R. 354 (Can.).

- Note that country names are always abbreviated (e.g., Can. for Canada; Colom. for Colombia; Guat. for Guatemala).
- S.C.R. refers to the Supreme Court of Canada (note that every country has different names for courts).

International Materials

Treaty of Friendship, Commerce and Navigation, U.S.-Japan, art. X, Apr. 2, 1953, 4. U.S.T. 2063.

- Note that this is an example of a bilateral treaty citation (can be applied to free trade agreements or bilateral investment treaties as well).

Geneva Convention Relative to the Treatment of Prisoners of War art. 3, Aug. 12, 1949, 6 U.S.T. 3316, 75 U.N.T.S. 135.

- Note this is an example of a multilateral treaty, including two source references for the treaty.
- Military and Paramilitary Activities (Nicar. v. U.S.), 1986 I.C.J. 14 (June 27).
- Note that this is an example of an International Court of Justice case.

Calderón v. Colombia, Case 10.454, Inter-Am. C.H.R., Report No. 32/92, OEA/Ser.L./V/II.83, doc. 14, corr. 1 (1992-93).

- Note that this is an example of a case from the Inter-American Court of Human Rights.

Structuring a Citation

A citation can be in-line with the text ("in-text citations") or it can be a footnote to the text. Unless a rule of the court specifies otherwise, either method is appropriate, but footnotes are preferable.

Romer v. Evans, 517 U.S. 620, 633 (1996) (arguing that the Colorado amendment violated the equal protection clause).

- Unless it is apparent why you are including a citation, an explanatory parenthetical should be included after the citation.
- Always begin an explanatory parenthetical with a gerund (i.e., a word ending in — ing).
- Alternatively, you may use a direct quote as your explanatory parenthetical, which does not require the use of a gerund to begin the quote.

Note that you can find additional BlueBook tips from the BlueBook website at: https://www.legalbluebook.com/Public/BlueTips.aspx.

[C] TECHNOLOGY AND CITATION

Getting a copy of the BlueBook to keep on your desk is a wise idea if you plan to do legal writing for a U.S. audience. However, you can also leverage technology to help ensure that you are properly citing your sources. One of the most well-known solutions to citation is a software package called "Endnote."

Endnote is a source collection database that allows you to enter all of your information about sources and store them in a database online or on your computer. Then, it automatically formats those sources in any style that you need, including APA (used for most social science writing) and, since 2007, BlueBook (used for all legal writing). In addition, Endnote integrates with MS Word on your computer, allowing you to quickly insert your legal citations in the proper format while you prepare your legal memoranda or other document.

Endnote is not the only product that automatically formats citations, but it is one of the easiest to use. You can learn more about it here: http://endnote.com/.

Chapter 9

EDITING AND FINALIZING YOUR DRAFT

The time to begin writing an article is when you have finished it to your satisfaction. By that time you begin to clearly and logically perceive what it is you really want to say.[37]

[A] INTRODUCTION

No matter the type of document being drafted, it is imperative that an author leave time for editing and proofreading. This last step in the process helps to significantly eliminate minor mistakes and facilitate smooth reading. In this chapter, we will cover the best techniques in properly editing and proofreading a document, including through the use of external services.

Topics Covered in This Chapter:

- The Importance of Editing
- Using Technology to Facilitate the Editing Process
- Professionally Sending Changes in Documents Electronically
- Key Editing Tricks and Tips
- Using Professional Editing Services

"All writers need editors, whether it's you, or me, or F. Scott Fitzgerald. There are two reasons: The first is that people tend to fall in love with their own prose. It's part of human nature. And so they don't want to change it. The second reason is that when I write something, I know what I'm trying to say. So when I read it over, I don't see what isn't clear because I already know what I'm trying to say. So I need someone who doesn't know what I was trying to say to raise questions. I'm not saying you have to go out and hire an editor. You can team up with other people in the office. Editing is one of the keys to the writing process and you just can't short-circuit it. But lawyers often do, and it shows."[38]

Whether you are editing your own work or the work of a colleague, your time is being well spent. In most cases, it takes less effort to write a legal document than it

---

[37] *Mark Twain's Notebook*, 1902-1903.

[38] Steven Stark, *Interview: Win Cases with Effective Writing, Be Concise; Avoid Adjectives and Archaic Terms*, Plain Language Association International, *available at* http://www.plainlanguagenetwork.org/legal/stark.html (accessed on September 29, 2012).

does to edit it. This is because the editing process requires you to assess a document for not only grammatical and stylistic issues, but also for meaning and effectiveness. Editing will turn an ordinary legal document into a convincing and powerful piece of legal prose.

[B] STEP 1: GRAMMAR AND STYLE EDITING

When you have a completed document in front of you and are ready to begin the editing process, first determine whether you will proceed using technology or traditional methods (e.g., pen and paper). If you plan to use traditional methods, it is wise to become familiar with proofing marks used in the publishing industry. There are a plethora of marks available to indicate any change you want to make to the text; however, as many legal writers are unfamiliar with more specialized marks, I recommend using only the most common marks, which can be found in the image below.

His account is in arears.	A caret indicates that a letter should be added.
The client pled guilty. (pleaded)	A strikethrough line with a caret indicates that a word should be removed and replaced with another.
The judge appeared angry, and frustrated with the prosecutor.	A strikethrough line indicates that a letter, word, phrase, or punctuation should be removed.
How often do Courts take on political cases like this?	A line through an upper case letter indicates that it should be set in lower case.
The opinion from the Supreme court was delivered today.	Three lines under a lower case letter means that it should be set in upper case.
The defendant wants to file a habeas corpus petition. (ital.)	A line under a word or the "ital.." text mean to italicize the word or phrase.
The client intentionally misled her attorney.	A line under a word with dashes through it indicates that an underline should be removed.
I can not believe that the judge dismissed the case!	These marks indicate that two words should be unified.
Howmany arbitrators will sit on the panel?	A single line between letters indicates that a space should be added.
Did the defendant plead guilty really?	This mark means that the words should be transposed.
The agency had full authority to issue the regulation. (stet)	"Stet" means to ignore the editor's mark and revert to the original text.

If you prefer to edit on the computer, you will most likely be using Track Changes, a feature of Microsoft Word. Before you begin making any edits, be sure that you have turned on the Track Changes function. From that point on, every change that you make to the document, whether to text or formatting, will be highlighted for the writer.

If you are editing a document that already has track change edits from other reviewers or if you dislike the distraction of colorful lines and highlights that appear when track changes is activated, consider selecting the option in the track changes toolbar for "Final." Switching to final view will continue recording all changes made to the document but will not reveal them to you on the screen. When you have completed your edits, you can switch on "Final: Show Markup" to see the changes that you made to the original document.

As you proceed through this first stage of editing, you will be addressing issues such as spelling, word choice, gender and number agreement, style, punctuation, and citations. Be sure to focus on the common errors that legal writers make, including:

- Over-capitalization
- Improper use of acronyms and initialisms (i.e., words or names are not properly spelled-out the first time they are used)
- Failure to transition between sentences/ paragraphs
- Inconsistency between person or gender
- Verbosity
- Ambiguity and abstract concepts
- Failure to use Plain English

[C] STEP 2: SUBSTANTIVE EDITING

Once you have a clean document to review, and after you have thoroughly read it for grammar and style errors, you will be in the right mindset to review for substance. The message of the document should be apparent to you at this point. If it is not, or if you are unable to fully understand the purpose of the document, you may want to start by meeting with (or calling) the writer to get some additional details about the intent. If the writer has failed to convey clearly his or her purpose in drafting the document, the intended recipient will either fail to respond at all or question the purpose/value of the document.

For your substantive review, ask the following questions about the document:

- Is it written in language that the intended recipient will understand?
- Does it include enough supporting authority to be convincing?
- Is it free of opinion and conjecture?
- Is the issue stated at the outset resolved through the analysis?
- Does the conclusion logically follow the analysis?
- Does the document leave you with any unanswered questions?
- Does the document include any unnecessary analysis?
- Will any statement create liability for the writer or the firm?

Your substantive review is akin to a due diligence analysis where you investigate the underlying quality concerns of a potential client or business. Here, you are ensuring that the document is complete yet not overly broad; succinct yet sufficiently detailed; and precise yet free of liability-creating statements. It may take you several reviews and some exchange with the author before the substantive review is complete.

If you are using track changes to edit the document, your substantive remarks should appear via the comment function. When you come across a sentence, phrase, or word that gives you cause for concern, highlight it and then, in the track changes toolbar, select "New Comment." This will highlight that portion of the text and link it to a comment bubble in the margin where you can convey your concern. This is a productive way to interact with the author as they can respond to your comments as they are addressed in the review process.

Before we leave behind the editing process, there is one final tool that you would be wise to become familiar with. Within the track changes toolbar, you have an option to compare documents. This feature allows the user to take two similar documents and to ask MS Word to identify the differences between the two. This is particularly valuable in two instances:

- Version Control: If you have multiple versions of the same document and you are not quite sure which one is which because someone edited the document without using track changes, you can open two versions with the compare tool and identify the differences quickly and easily.
- Verification: If you are exchanging electronic drafts of a document with a client or third party, they may send it back to you with minor changes without having recorded them in track changes. A good lawyer always runs the new version against the one that was originally sent to ensure that they are aware of every "minor" change.

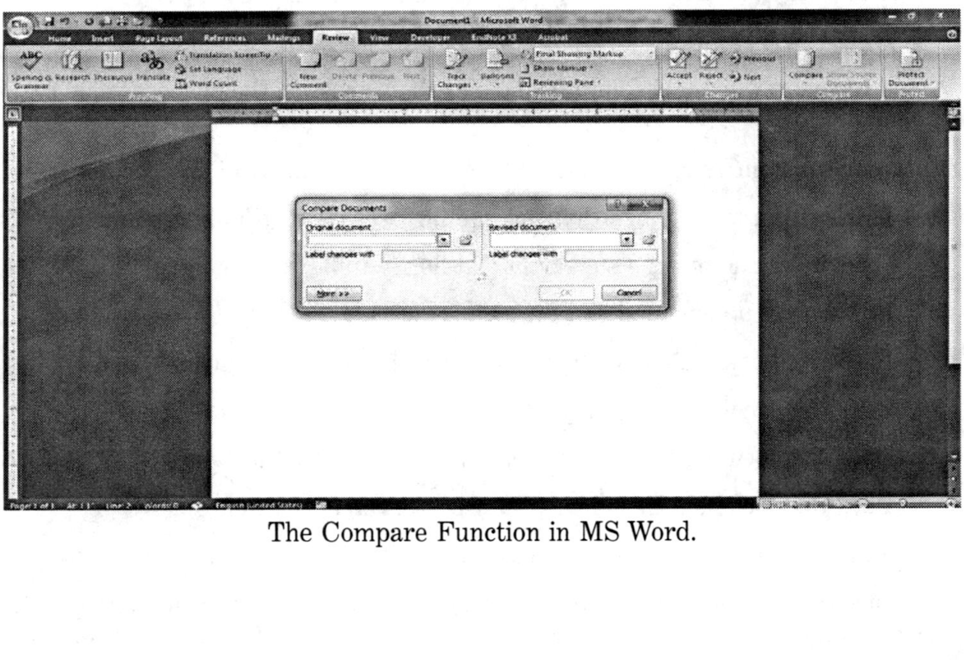

The Compare Function in MS Word.

EXERCISE: EDITING A LETTER

Review the following draft letter of intent between two oil and gas companies. Edit the document using the track changes function of MS Word or the editing marks discussed above.

Dear Canadian Gas, Co.

This letter of Intent compleats our sale to the Canadian Gas, Company ("buyer") by Ukraine Oil, Inc. (the "Seller") of the Sellers business (the "Company"), located in Kiev, The Ukraine. The partys agreed to a enforceable agreement (the "Agreement") of the purchase of the Acquired Company by the Seller to the Buyer. If the Buyer agrees to this letter, then the parties will sign in the future an Agreement that will show the terms in this letter of intent..

Terms:

The Purchaser will buy the Company, and include all equipment, current and passed contracts, and all documents, and files and records on the Business. The Buyer will take on the duties of the operation of the Company after the closing date. Purchase Price. The purchase price will be $500,000,000.00. The partys must tell third parties with outstanding contracts that the company has been sold. The Seller will run the Company as they have in the past. The Buyer and the Seller will satisfy any duties still in the Agreement to third partys. The Seller agrees to participate with the Buyer's due diligence investigation of the Acquired Company and to provide the Buyer and its representatives with immediate access to critical employees and to all records pertaining to the Acquired Company.

The Buyer will get information from Seller on the Company and will use this information only for researching and confirming that the Company is as the Seller told the Buyer. All information must remain confidential.

Beginning today and until December 31, 2012, the Seller will not sign any contract with outside corporations to sell their Company. If the Buyer does not buy the Company, then the Buyer will pay Seller a service fee equaling 3% of the purchase price. All other expenses will be paid by each respective party.

If you agree with this letter of intent agreement, please sign it and and return a to our New York Office within 5 days. We will then sign the agreement to sell the company.

Sincerely,

____

Ukraine Oil, Inc.

A Sample Revised Letter can be found in Appendix A.

Chapter 10

CONCLUDING POINTS

In an interview with humorist David Sedaris a few years ago, Sedaris said, "Writing gives you the illusion of control, and then you realize it's just an illusion, that people are going to bring their own stuff into it."[39] I don't imagine he was speaking about legal writing in particular, but his words resonate in our profession and neatly summarize the point that I would like to leave you with.

You have a responsibility as a legal writer greater than that of most other writers. You have a responsibility to your client, to your firm or organization, to the legal profession, and to yourself. A lawyer's words carry the weight of authority with them. They encourage people to take actions they might not normally take, or to avoid acting when they otherwise would. While the words of a fiction writer are meant to be enjoyed, and the words of a science writer are meant to illuminate, the words of a lawyer are meant to be followed.

Your words, whether spoken or written, create a legacy for you as their conveyor. Whether they motivate or prevent a certain action, they are binding you to the results. If a client reads your opinion letter and concludes that he or she should take a certain action, and that action leads to negative consequences, that client will hold you responsible. And despite your best effort to explain that the client misinterpreted your words, you will be bound to the dispute.

What we write as lawyers is usually our best interpretation of the law or a legal issue. We are not (despite what some may espouse) all-knowing, able to predict the future, or infallible. In fact, and this may be hard to accept, there are instances in which we are wrong. In those instances, we are not called by our editor to prepare an updated version of our article or book; we are not asked to print a correction in the next Sunday newspaper. We are often notified via a complaint filed by our former client who took our words as gospel and placed his or her trust in us as legal counsel. Our opportunity to correct what we wrote may be in a courtroom, where we need our own defense counsel.

As Sedaris said, writing gives us the illusion of control. We believe that we are directing the actions we want our client or colleagues or third-parties to take, and we believe that our words will make them act in the way that we want. We expect our demand letter to convince a third-party to cease trespassing on our client's property. We expect that our legal memorandum will convince a partner to accept a case. We expect that our contract will protect our client and convince the other party to act in

[39] David Sedaris, Interview in Louisville Courier-Journal, June 5, 2005.

accordance with its terms. Unfortunately, our words sometimes fail us.

Writers often write with the expectation that their reader will think like them. They often assume that the reader has the same amount of experience with the issue, knowledge of the language, and understanding of the importance of what is being written about. While this may be true on occasion, it is more often the case that the reader is less informed or less interested than the writer assumes. This means that a poorly crafted letter, memo, or contract can easily be incorrectly understood by the reader. And since the reader is expected to act upon those words, the action may not be what the writer intended.

So should we lower our expectations of reader knowledge and oversimplify all of our writing? No. As legal professionals, we have been given the training and tools necessary to critically assess issues, predict outcomes, and persuade parties to act. Our words are weapons and, when wielded properly, can cut through any combative legal issue. Dulling our blades will not help us to achieve our mission.

Instead, we must take pains to anticipate how our words will be used and predict the impact that any actions based on our words will have on us, our firm or organization, or the public. We can accomplish this with two simple steps. First, we should ask with every sentence — with every word even — whether it is necessary. Over-explanation and expansive verbiage leads to confusion, misinterpretation, and often creates liability for us. Make a concerted effort with every document to include only what is absolutely essential and nothing more. Save your lengthy explanations for journal articles and opinion pieces in the press.

Second, read every sentence as if you were the intended recipient of the document. What action would you consider taking based upon those words? Assume that every sentence might be misinterpreted. Would a reasonable misinterpretation lead to an action that you don't intend? If so, rewrite or eliminate the sentence. This is easier said than done. A writer often has a difficult time disconnecting themselves from the author-perspective. However, mastering this skill will undoubtedly lead to more effective legal writing and, perhaps even more importantly, limited liability for you and your firm or organization.

In this short book, I have attempted to provide you with the framework for understanding, as a foreign law student or legal practitioner, how to effectively communicate legal concepts in English. As you continue to develop and refine your legal writing skills, you will establish certain habits that guide your writing for the rest of your career. These habits, if based upon the lessons in this and related guidebooks on legal style, will make you an outstanding legal writer and a more successful legal advocate.

I encourage you to spend every day making efforts to improve your legal writing, whether by offering to edit or proofread a colleague's document, writing an article for a law journal, or briefing a case. A law degree does not signify that we have reached the summit of our legal education; it means that we are prepared to begin the journey. Keep practicing, keep learning, and never doubt for a moment that, in this profession, your words are what will make you great.

Appendix A:

SOLUTIONS TO EXERCISES

[A] AMBIGUOUS DRAFTING EXERCISE

Recommended solutions to ambiguous drafting examples:

1. Explanation 1: It remains unclear whether "these" costs are all of the costs that the client must pay the attorney for his out-of-pocket expenses and if the four costs listed after "include" are exhaustive of the attorney's fees.
2. Explanation 2: It is ambiguous when Alfred will "come of age," as this usually indicates when a person becomes an adult, which is eighteen years old in the United States. This provision may be unenforceable as too ambiguous because the owner also stated that he would give the property to his son when the son turned twenty-one years old.
3. Explanation 3: The buyer does not know whether the property is located at East or West 55th Street in New York City.
4. Explanation 4: It is impracticable for a home owner to know what constitutes a "tall" tree, and whether any tree was planted before 1950 that is now growing on their property.
5. Explanation 5: And/or clauses are ambiguous when two options are presented and cannot both be completed.
6. Explanation 6: It is ambiguous as to who would be responsible for the loan. The court in *Ethridge v. Tier One Bank*, 226 S.W.3d 127, 131 (Mo. 2007) held that the wife would not be responsible because the bank failed to list her as a borrower on the loan.
7. Explanation 7: These two clauses are inconsistent because the company cannot claim to not be liable within the first 15 days of the policy period, but also have said that it is liable for disability injuries. The court held that these two clauses could not be reconciled and, citing Blackstone's Commentaries, that the first clause should be accepted and the second rejected. *See Drucker v. W. Indem. Co. of Dallas, Tex.*, 223 S.W. 989, 991 (Mo. App. E.D. 1920).
8. Explanation 8: The consequence of this language is that natural border markers can move, and the Blue River now extends two miles into the property that originally belonged to Nation B and Nation B will continue to lose land mass unless the two parties renegotiate and clarify their agreement.
9. Explanation 9: The ambiguity is both the United States and Canada use the monetary denomination of dollar, however, the American Dollar and the Canadian Dollar are valued at different rates.

10. Explanation 10: It is unknown what constitutes "educational equivalent," also, the semi-colon is misplaced and could be read to require (1) a college degree (or its educational equivalent) and (2) full time military service.

[B] SUPERFLUOUS LANGUAGE EXERCISE

1. The court in *United States v. Smith* held that Smith could deduct from his taxes any money that he stole and returned in the same year, but could not do so for funds stolen and repaid in subsequent years.
2. I received your letter dated July 25, 2012 about the *Spann* case and have enclosed my response. I look forward to your response.
3. I move to file a motion for summary judgment.
4. Seller agrees to sell 1000 stocks to buyer at $0.50 cents each.
5. The parties agree to fulfill all obligations contained in this contract.

[C] SENTENCE STRUCTURE EXERCISE

1. Answer 1: International Commercial Arbitration: the binding resolution of the merits between State X and MNE in regards to any right or obligation arising out of this Agreement. Each Party waives any right to adjudicate any dispute in any other court or forum. The Parties agree that all disputes arising out of the validity, interpretation, construction and performance of this Agreement will be filed and heard by the Permanent Court of Arbitration in The Hague, The Netherlands.
2. Answer 2: Royalty Income: All amounts collected by Licensor for registered and authorized use of artist's songs to Distributor, including but not limited to royalties for secondary or simultaneous retransmission by means of any radio, cable, satellite, Internet, or other electronic system. Licensor has the sole right to apply for and collect all these amounts. If Distributor receives any such amounts, Distributor will immediately remit them to Licensor with statement identifying their source.
3. Answer 3: Confidential Information: Subcontractor or its agents shall not disclose any proprietary information of the other party with respect to such other party, that may be in the possession of that party to any other party who is not a partner, officer, employee, counsel, or agent of such party except with written consent. Where information is distributed by Electronic Delivery, party will deliver materials to other party by electronic transmission over the Internet or comparable service. Parties hereby agree to obtain and use reasonable and commercially available digital rights management software to protect information contained within electronic delivery.
4. Answer 4: Material Adverse Change: The option of Buyer to exit negotiations without liability in the occurrence of any condition, change or development, including a downtown in the state's economy, that could reasonably be expected to have a material adverse effect on the business, assets, liabilities or operations.

[D] PARALLEL STRUCTURE EXERCISE

Suggested Solutions to the Parallel Structure Exercise:

1. Answer 1: Each Member hereby agrees to cooperate by executing and delivering in a timely fashion, any and all additional documents, including statements of interest and holdings, designations, powers of attorney and other instruments, necessary to effectuate and comply with the purposes of the Company and this Operating Agreement and any applicable laws, rules, or regulations.
2. Answer 2: In order to comply with the 2012 Judicial Sentencing Guidelines, the 2012 D.C. Superior Court Code was redrafted to include new sections on ten additional offenses, remedial measures for victims of violent crime, and enhanced penalties.
3. Answer 3: The seller must act reasonably and in good faith. Such general terminology provides neither the seller nor the buyer with an understanding of potential causes of action or mechanisms for recovery.

[E] VOICE EXERCISE

1. Active 1: They will convey the fee-simple interest to the defendant.
2. Active 2: The plaintiff demonstrated that she had paid the defendant for his interest in the promissory note.
3. Active 3: The judge sanctioned the lawyer for misappropriating client funds.
4. Active 4: By signing this contract, buyer agrees to all conditions.
5. Active 5: Seller will deliver the parcels after payment.
6. Active 6: Buyer accepts items in their current condition.
7. Active 7: The contractor will have constructed the embassy by November.
8. Active 8: Lessor will rent the parcel for a reasonable price.
9. Active 9: The coast guard discovered that someone stole the cargo from the ship. (Better in passive voice)
10. Active 10: Any party will not exceed the term length for any reason. (Better in passive voice)

[F] FRAMING THE ISSUE EXERCISE

EXERCISE 1: CLIENT JOHNSON ISSUE STATEMENT

Issue: Whether client would be able to keep his Picasso painting, entitled "Last Realm," over the claims of the bankruptcy creditors of the art dealer, Sam Beekman, whom he contacted to sell his painting on consignment.

Johnson delivered his painting to Beekman on sale or return, at his store on December 1, 2009. Beekman filed for Chapter 7 bankruptcy on January 1, 2010, thus rendering the painting as inventory, and thereafter transferring the painting to Beekman after the commencement and during the pendency of his bankruptcy case. The painting was transferred to Beekman, according to the court, because under Chapter 7 Bankruptcy, the court-appointed trustee may take possession of the business, including all items in inventory. Johnson's painting would be considered an "item in inventory" at the time of the Chapter 7 action because the painting was not returned to him.

The statutory provisions of the Franklin Commercial Code (FCC) § 2-326 control in review of the conflicting language of the consignment contract between Johnson and Beekman. This means that the FCC provides that even if an agreement purports to reserve title to the person making delivery until payment or resale, or uses such words as "on consignment," the "sale or return of goods," will be subject to buyer's creditor's claims while in the buyer's possession. (FCC § 2-326 (1) (b) and (2)). For a good to be deemed on "sale or return," the good must be delivered primarily for resale, and delivered to a person for sale at a place of business at which the buyer deals in goods of the kind involved, under a name other than the name of the person making the delivery. Because Johnson delivered his painting to Beekman on sale or return, at his store, which is a store dealing primarily in the sale of pieces of art consigned by artists, then his painting would be deemed to be fall within the designation of goods delivered primarily for resale.

Although Johnson's painting is considered to qualify as an asset of the bankruptcy estate under the Bankruptcy Act, Chapter 7 Bankruptcy, and the FCC, the FCC has carved out exceptions to allow for certain consignors to retain full possession of their consigned items during the existence of a consignee's bankruptcy action. Johnson can lawfully retain his painting, the "Last Realm," because he has potentially satisfied his burden of proof under the defenses of FCC § 2-326(3) by posting a sign on the back of his painting to retain consignor's interest; and by establishing that Beekman is generally known to his creditors as a person substantially engaged in selling goods of others.

Under the first defense within FCC § 2-326(3), he will likely be found to have complied with an applicable law providing for a consignor's interest or the like to be evidence by a sign. The applicable law is FCC § 3533, which states that a person who transacts business must identify his place of business with a sign in letters easy to read and posted conspicuously to state that he is in dealing in property in which others have an interest and all property used in such business must be identified. In order to conclusively determine whether Beekman has fulfilled this obligation, it will be necessary to visit his store and see whether there is a clearly-lettered and conspicuous sign posted on the front door that Beekman mentioned to his in his interview that stated, "All offers will be considered and forwarded to the artists."

In addition, the statute requires that every item be identified within his store. The statute does not clearly define whether the identification on each item must also be with letters easy to read and posted conspicuously, however, it is likely that the tag he placed on the back of the painting will fulfill this requirement. In the persuasive case of *In re Merry*, the United States District Court of the Eastern District of New York Court held that if the consignor could have shown that the cards posted on consigned goods for sale did in fact impart such knowledge on the consignee's creditors, to such an extent that it was "generally known" by the creditors, and that the cards also suggested that the consignee was "substantially engaged" in selling goods not owned by him, then the sign(s) would fulfill the requirements. However, the court held that the imparting knowledge to the customers was not be dispositive in proving that the creditors knew of the consignor's interest, and thus could be find irrelevant in this matter. It is arguable that the signs he posted on the back of his painting would be found to be imparting knowledge to customers as opposed to creditors. However, the creditors may be found to have "generally known" that the consignee was in the business of selling property of others if all or most of the items for sale were from consignors. (*See In re Merry*). Johnson stated that he believed that most of the items Beekman was displaying in his store were on consignment, thus this defense may be fulfilled with this fact.

It will be necessary to research more case law on this issue and whether Beekman did/does in fact sell items on consignment for all or most of the artwork on display in his store. We will find this information by asking Beekman and reviewing his other business contracts and inventory.

EXERCISE 2: CLIENT LOCKETT ISSUE STATEMENT

Issue 1: Who are possible Defendants in this case? Why?

There are three possible Defendants: George McConnell, Tropics North, and the Miami reptile supplier.

Lockett has three causes of action for professional negligence against McConnell. First, McConnell failed to provide adequate training, supervision or warning of risk to Lockett. Second, McConnell did not ensure that the area containing the snakes was secure. Third, as an exotic pet store owner, McConnell did not use reasonable care in administering emergency first aid to Lockett. Because McConnell is an agent of Tropics North, the store can be held liable for McConnell's actions.

Under 15 U.S.C. § 8089, a shipper licensed by the Interstate Commerce Commission must indicate on the bill of lading and freight cartons the dangerous nature of the contained animal. It is uncertain whether *Philodryas viridissimus* is venomous. As reptile suppliers, the Miami distributors had a duty to know about the uncertainty of the snake's classification. They failed to warn McConnell of the potential danger of the snake, thus violating the 15 U.S.C. § 8089. The Miami reptile supplier was negligent in failing to inform McConnell about the possibility that the snake was venomous.

Issue 2: In what court and in what state should the suit be brought?

MARYLAND:

The suits against McConnell, Tropics North, and the Miami supplier could be brought in Maryland. Maryland state courts have subject-matter jurisdiction. Based on the facts, Maryland courts can exercise general personal jurisdiction over McConnell, and Tropics North. Maryland is an appropriate venue because a significant amount of the events from which the claim arises occurred in Maryland.

Under the Maryland Long-Arm Statute, the Miami reptile supplier is subject to Maryland specific personal jurisdiction. Md. Code Ann. § 6-102 (1999). The suit could be brought in Maryland federal court based on diversity jurisdiction. Diversity Jurisdiction is satisfied because the Plaintiff and Defendants are domiciled in separate states and the matter at issue exceeds $75,000.

FLORIDA:

Since damages are not awarded in Maryland if Lockett is found guilty of contributory negligence, Florida is a better state to bring suit against McConnell, Tropics North, and the Miami supplier. The suits against McConnell, Tropics North, and the Miami supplier could be brought in Florida. Florida can exercise general personal jurisdiction over the Miami supplier because they conduct systematic and continuous business in Florida. *International Shoe Co. v. Washington*, 326 U.S. 310, 320 (1945).

Florida has specific personal jurisdiction over McConnell and Tropics North because it is reasonable and because they have minimal contacts in Florida. Jurisdiction over the Defendants is not unreasonable because it does not offend "traditional conception[s] of fair play and substantial justice embodied in the Due Process Clause of the Fourteenth Amendment." *International Shoe Co. v. Washington*, 326 U.S. 310, 320 (1945). The burden on McConnell and Tropics North is higher if tried in Florida because they have no physical connection to Florida.

The Florida Statute § 372.90 was developed to regulate the transportation of exotic pets. This demonstrates that Florida has a high public interest in adjudicating because the Miami reptile supplier sells throughout Florida and nationwide. Under Florida statute § 372.90, Lockett may have a cause for private action to sue the Miami supplier. When balancing all these factors, the burden on McConnell and Tropics North does not outweigh the Plaintiff's interest and Florida's interest in adjudicating. Even if McConnell's contacts do not justify specific personal jurisdiction, the suit can be heard in the Federal Court under supplemental jurisdiction according to 28 U.S.C. § 1367. The omission giving rise to the claim occurred in Miami by the supplier; therefore Florida is an acceptable venue under the 28 Federal Rules of Civil Procedure § 1391. The case can be brought in federal court under diversity Jurisdiction because the Plaintiff and Defendants are domiciled in separate states and the matter at issue exceeds $75,000.

[G] APPLYING SOURCES OF LAW EXERCISE

Each of the sources of law found for the Lockett case is explained below.

1. *Heath v. Swift Wings*, 252 S.E.2d 526 (N.C. App. 1979). This case is primary authority but it is persuasive only since it is from another state. However, it is valuable because we can conclude based on this case that McConnell, as the owner and manager of Tropics North, failed to exercise the degree of care required by members of his profession.

2. *International Shoe Co. v. Washington*, 326 U.S. 310 (1945). As a U.S. Supreme Court case, this is binding authority on all courts. Based on the facts in this case, Maryland courts can exercise general personal jurisdiction over

McConnell, Tropics North and the physicians because their contact with the state is "systematic and continuous," *International Shoe* at 320, and because McConnell could be personally served in Maryland. Florida can exercise general personal jurisdiction over the Miami supplier because they conduct systematic and continuous business in Florida.

3. *Ortiz v. Animal Exotique Boutique*, 66 A.2d 587 (N.C. 2011). As a North Carolina state appeals court case, this decision is persuasive authority for us. Initially, this decision seems contrary to our client's case; however, if we distinguish our exotic bright green snake from an average snake, we may be able to make an exception to the rule established here. We want to pursue damages under the theory that the exotic animal had a dangerous propensity and the pet store owner can be found strictly liable by having assumed the risk of selling dangerous animals.

4. *World-Wide Volkswagen Corp. v. Woodson*, 444 U.S. 286 (1980). This is another U.S. Supreme Court case, which makes it binding authority on all courts. This case establishes that a single instance of contact with a state is not likely sufficient to constitute minimum contacts and thus establish personal jurisdiction. However, our case seems to involve a supplier that routinely sent pets to the Maryland store. We can use World-Wide Volkswagen to establish that it is constitutional to exercise specific personal jurisdiction over the Miami supplier because the claim arises out of their minimal contacts with Maryland. Since the supplier regularly does business with McConnell and derives substantial revenue from goods used in Maryland, the supplier meets the jurisdictional requirements.

5. *Haggard v. Ritsick*, 47 N.E.2d 33 (Mass. 2009). This case is not favorable to our client. However, as a Massachusetts case, it serves only as persuasive authority and will carry less weight in a Maryland court. This case will most likely be cited by McConnell, Tropic North and the Miami supplier because it defends their position that they are not liable for injuries to customers while they are handling the pets for sale in the store.

6. *Asahi Metal Industry v. Superior Court*, 480 U.S. 102 (1987). This is another U.S. Supreme Court case and thus applies as binding authority on all courts. This case does not prevent us from acquiring jurisdiction over the Miami supplier. The sales of exotic pets by the Miami supplier to the Maryland pet store likely establish sufficient minimum contact to overcome any defense against personal jurisdiction.

7. *Burger King Corp. v. Rudzewicz*, 471 U.S. 462 (1985). McConnell and Tropics North purposefully availed themselves in Florida by entering into multiple contracts with the Miami supplier, thus satisfying the required minimal contacts standard for specific personal jurisdiction.

8. *Iguana Pet Store v. State of Florida*, 55 So.3d 1475 (Fla. Dist. Ct. App. 2010). If we file our complaint in Florida, this case will be binding authority on the court. However, as the Miami supplier did have a license to ship the snake to Tropics North, we will not be able to notify the state that they violated any

laws regarding shipping or dealing in exotic pets, making this precedent less valuable.

[H] EDITING A LETTER OF INTENT EXERCISE

Dear [insert representative's name]:

This letter of intent completes our agreement on the terms of the sale to the Canadian Gas Company (the "Buyer") by Ukraine Oil, Inc. ("Seller") of the Seller's business ("Acquired Company"), located in Kiev, Ukraine. Through this agreement, the parties commence the negotiation of an enforceable agreement ("Acquisition Agreement"). The parties agree to prepare and execute an Acquisition Agreement that reflects the terms set forth in this letter of intent.

The Acquisition Agreement shall include the following terms:

At the closing, Purchaser will purchase all of the assets associated with the Acquired Company, including all current accounts, all outstanding contracts, all equipment, and all documents, files and records regarding the Acquired Company.

Buyer will assume as of the closing date only those obligations resulting from the operation of the Acquired Company accruing after the closing date.

Purchase Price. The purchase price will be US$500,000,000, payable via electronic wire transfer.

The parties will inform all third parties with outstanding contracts relating to the operations of the Acquired Company of the potential sale and will use all reasonable efforts to acquire necessary third-party consent.

Seller agrees to participate with Buyer's due diligence investigation of the Acquired Company and to provide Buyer and its representatives with immediate access to critical employees and to all records pertaining to the Acquired Company. Buyer will use the due diligence information solely for the purpose of Buyer's due diligence investigation of the Acquired Company. Buyer remains liable for any breach of confidentiality regarding the due diligence report or information about the sale and purchase of the Acquired Company. The provisions of this paragraph will survive the termination of this letter of intent.

Until December 31, 2012, Seller will not enter into any agreement or discussion with any other corporation regarding the possible disposition of a material portion of the Acquired Company, or any business involving the oil and gas industries.

If the Acquired Company is not acquired by Buyer within 90 days of the date of this letter of intent, Buyer will pay to Seller a service fee equaling 3% of the purchase price, and Seller's expenses in connection with the negotiation of the acquisition. All other costs, including legal fees, incurred in connection with the acquisition of the Acquired Company will be paid by each respective party.

If you are in agreement with the terms of this letter, please execute this letter of intent and return a signed copy to our New York Office within five business days of receipt. Upon receipt of a signed copy of this letter, we will proceed with negotiation and drafting of the Acquisition Agreement.

Sincerely,

Ukraine Oil, Inc.

By:________________________ Date signed: ____________
[Name and Title]

Canadian Gas, Co.

By: ________________________ Date signed: ____________
[Name and Title]

Appendix B:

SAMPLE DOCUMENTS

[A] SAMPLE OPINION LETTER

Mr. George Jones
General Counsel
Intech Enterprise, Inc.
300 South Market Street
San Jose, California 95113
USA

September 22, 2011

Re: Joint Venture in Beijing, China

Dear Mr. Jones:

I am providing this opinion to you pursuant to your inquiry about whether your company, Intech Enterprise, Inc. ("Intech"), would be permitted to execute a joint venture agreement with my client, Global Communications, Ltd. ("GC"), under Chinese commercial law. This opinion letter is delivered to you regarding the potential joint venture and may not be relied on for any other purpose.

After examining the relevant documents, and based upon our foregoing discussions, I am of the opinion that Intech may proceed under Chinese commercial law with drafting and executing a Joint Venture Agreement to commence international financial transactions between Intech and GC according to the terms of the previously agreed upon International Trade Documents. This opinion is subject to the following assumptions:

1. Intech validly, currently and actively exists as a corporation in good standing under Delaware law.

2. Intech has registered their name with the Ministry of Commerce of the People's Republic of China as a foreign corporation.

3. Intech is not a party to any pending action known to me that may adversely affect the transactions contemplated by the International Trade Documents or that may have a material adverse effect on Intech or GC.

4. Intech has duly authorized, executed and delivered the International Trade Documents in which it is named as a party, and such International Trade Documents constitute its interest in establishing a joint venture with GC. The execution and delivery of the International Trade Documents and the fulfillment by Intech of the terms of the joint venture do not conflict with or breach any corporate documents of

Intech, GC, or any law, regulation, or regulatory body having jurisdiction over Intech or GC.

5. Intech has the legal authority to enter into and perform contractual obligations under applicable Chinese commercial laws.

6. Intech has filed and successfully obtained all necessary authorizations, licenses and permits required by the Chinese federal authorities to engage in the transactions described by the International Trade Documents.

If you have any further questions, please do not hesitate to contact my office. Thank you.

Sincerely,
Lin Xiaoping
General Counsel
Global Communications, Ltd.

[B] SAMPLE DEMAND LETTER

Mr. Robert Duzinpay
1020 Lazyman Road
Allentown, PA 18029

June 15, 2012

Re: Case No. 8019 (Duzinpay)

Dear Mr. Duzinpay,

On February 20, 2012, you visited my law office located in Allentown, Pennsylvania. During that visit, you signed a retainer agreement with my firm whereby you consented to provide payment for legal services rendered pursuant to your claim against your former employer, Tefloni, Inc. At the conclusion of that meeting, you asked that we begin investigating possible legal actions against Tefloni immediately, which we did.

On March 15, 2012, our firm sent you a letter outlining the potential legal claims that you could bring against your employer and offering you an in-person or telephone meeting to discuss which claim, if any, you preferred to pursue. You did not respond to that letter.

On April 1, 3, and 5, representatives from our firm called you and left voice messages at your home and office requesting a callback. On April 15, having received no further communications from you, we issued a final invoice for services rendered between February 20 and April 5. The total amount due was $725 and payment was due within 30 days of your receipt of the letter.

Since the letter was sent on April 15, 60 days have passed and payment has not yet been received. With this demand letter, I wish to remind you that this payment is still outstanding and to inform you that if payment is not received by July 15, we will be forced to file legal action with the Pennsylvania Superior Court.

You can prevent this legal action by making your full payment immediately. Payment arrangements can be made directly through our main office by calling (901) 555-5729. Thank you for your prompt attention to this matter.

Sincerely,

John Bennett, Managing Partner
Bennett and Silvers, LLC
600 Westlake Terrace
Allentown, PA 18001

[C] SAMPLE CASE BRIEF # 1

Rodriguez-Fernandez v. Wilkinson, 505 F. Supp. 787 (D. Kan. 1980).

Issue: Whether refugees can invoke protection from the U.S. Constitution?

Action: Petition for writ of habeas corpus.

Factual and Procedural History:

Petitioner was incarcerated in Cuba. The Government of Cuba sent him to the United States as a part of the Freedom Flotilla on a boat with approximately 130,000 Cuban nationals. Cuba barred petitioner from re-entry. Rodriquez-Fernandez sought admission to the United States as a refugee. The Immigration and Naturalization Service (INS) held him in federal prison while trying to classify him as a refugee, deportable, excludable or excluded alien. Petitioner asserts that his continued detention is cruel and unusual punishment in contravention of the 8th and 5th Amendments to the U.S. Constitution and in violation of customs of fundamental human justice as embodied in established principles of international law.

Analysis:

Although petitioner has no rights to avoid detention under either the 5th or 8th Amendments to the U.S. Constitution, the indeterminate detention of petitioner in a maximum security federal prison under conditions providing less freedom than that granted to ordinary inmates constitutes arbitrary detention and is a violation of customary international law. Customary international law demands the protection of these individuals from arbitrary detention. Principles of customary international law may be discerned from an overview of express international conventions, the teachings of legal scholars, the general custom and practice of nations and relevant judicial decisions. When from this overview a wrong is found to be of mutual, and not merely several, concern among nations, it may be termed an international law violation. The right or protection from indeterminate detention under customary international law is more important than imprisonment on a presumption of guilt based on Cuban law. Extended, indefinite confinement in a federal prison is deleterious to the personal integrity of petitioner and can only be viewed as an arbitrary decision.

Order:

Rodriguez-Fernandez has to be released from federal prison within ninety days. There are several means by which petitioner can be released: (1) he may be deported, (2) he may be released on parole, (3) the INS may conduct a "procedurally-adequate hearing" to determine whether he should be detained longer, (4) he can be transferred to a refugee camp for housing purposes, or (5) respondent can propose a suitable resolution. If the arbitrary detention of petitioner is not terminated to this court's satisfaction within ninety days, then this court will grant the petitioner's writ of habeas corpus and order him to be released on parole.

[D] SAMPLE CASE BRIEF #2

Gul v. Obama, 652 F.3d 12 (D.C. Cir. 2011).

Issue: Whether the petitions of Gul and Hamad, appellants, are not moot and whether the district court made certain procedural errors in reaching the contrary conclusion?

Action: Petitions for writ of habeas corpus.

Factual and Procedural History:

Pakistani forces arrested Hamad in Pakistan in 2002, and U.S. forces arrested Gul in Afghanistan in 2003. Both men were handed over to the U.S., labeled "enemy combatants" and transferred to the Naval Base at Guantanamo Bay, where they were held for several years. During their detention, both men filed petitions with the D.C. District Court for writs of habeas corpus seeking their immediate release. In 2007, the U.S. notified Gul and Hamad that they had been "approved to leave Guantanamo," but they may still be considered to be "enemy combatants." Gul was then transferred to Afghanistan in March 2007, and the D.C. District Court *sua sponte* dismissed his petition as moot. Gul promptly moved for reconsideration, but his motion was not immediately addressed. Hamad was transferred to the Sudan in December 2007. The D.C. District Court also did not resolve his motion, until 2008, when the U.S. Supreme Court issued *Boumediene v. Bush*, 553 U.S. 723 (2008). Pursuant to *Boumediene*, the D.C. District Court consolidated proceedings in all Guantanamo Bay cases and ordered all former detainees who had been transferred out of Guantanamo, but who still had habeas petitions pending, to submit a consolidated brief addressing the issue of mootness. On April 1, 2010, the D.C. District Court dismissed as moot all cases captioned in the consolidated brief, including the petitions of Gul and Hamad, because they were no longer being held by the U.S. Government and therefore the claim was beyond the court's jurisdiction under Article III of the Constitution. *See In re Petitioners Seeking Habeas Corpus Relief in Relation to Prior Detentions at Guantanamo Bay*, 700 F. Supp. 2d 119, 137 (D.D.C. 2010). Appellants now argue that their petitions are not moot because they continue to be burdened by the collateral consequences of their prior detention and continuing designation as "enemy combatants," specifically by suffering from travel restrictions, prohibition from entering the U.S., being subject to re-arrest, capture, detention and extrajudicial killing by the U.S., and having their reputations damaged.

Decision:

The D.C. Circuit Court affirmed the order of the lower court and found no merit in appellants' arguments that the D.C. District Court: (1) misapplied the collateral consequences doctrine, (2) improperly shifted the burden to appellants in requiring them to show their cases present a live controversy, (3) failed adequately to consider the facts of their individual cases, and (4) failed to abide by 28 U.S.C. § 2243, the statutory provision for a petition for writ of habeas corpus, that requires courts to dispose of a habeas petition as "law and justice require." The D.C. Circuit Court held that there was no presumption that former detainees faced collateral consequences sufficient to keep their habeas petitions from becoming moot upon their release from detention as designated "enemy combatants." The D.C. Circuit Court further held that the parties failed to make an actual showing that their prior detention or continued designation burdened them with concrete injuries. The D.C. Circuit Court concluded that injury to reputation is a secondary effect of an otherwise moot action, and the court requires some tangible concrete effect susceptible to judicial correction before it can assert jurisdiction, thus each former detainee failed to meet his burden of alleging facts that demonstrated he was a proper party to invoke judicial resolution of the dispute. The court was not required to consider, as an equitable factor, the fact that petitioners were denied a forum in which to bring their habeas petitions for a prolonged period before the Supreme Court assured them of one before dismissing their petitions as moot.

Order: Affirming the order of the District Court.

[E] SAMPLE OFFICE MEMORANDUM

OFFICE MEMORANDUM

To: Kevin Fandl, Firm Partner
From: Amy McQuade, Associate Attorney
Re: Andrea Johnson, private nuisance liability under the Massachusetts Spite Fence Statute
Date: July 1, 2012

QUESTION PRESENTED

Whether we should represent Ms. Andrea Johnson in her potential claim against her neighbors, the McKinneys, that they violated the Massachusetts Spite Fence Statute by constructing a fence that unnecessarily exceeds six feet in height, was maliciously erected or maintained for the purpose of annoying the adjacent neighbor, and injures Johnson's comfort in her estate, thus deeming the fence a private nuisance.

BRIEF ANSWER

No. We should not represent Johnson in this matter because she does not have a claim under the Massachusetts Spite Fence Statute as the fence it is not unnecessarily high, was not maliciously erected or maintained to annoy Johnson, and does not substantially interfere with Johnson's comfort in her estate.

First, a fence is unnecessarily high when the gravity of harm incurred by a neighbor outweighs the structure's utility. The McKinneys' fence is not unnecessarily high because it serves alternative purposes and Johnson's damages are minimal. Second, to classify a fence as maliciously erected, the dominant motive to build must be malice. The McKinneys' fence was not maliciously erected because their intent was to prevent further conflict with Johnson. Third, a fence injures the right to comfort when it substantially interferes with the neighbor's ordinary enjoyment of their property. The McKinneys' fence does not meet this benchmark because Johnson's injuries are not substantial. The McKinneys' fence is not a private nuisance because the fence does not satisfy three elements of the Spite Fence Statute and thus we should not represent her in this matter.

FACTS

Our potential client, Andrea Johnson of Sudbury, Massachusetts, requests our legal advice for an altercation with her next-door neighbors, Mr. and Mrs. McKinney. The McKinneys recently erected a twelve-foot wooden fence on the border of their and Johnson's properties. Johnson wants the court to order the removal of the fence because it obstructs the sunlight to Johnson inherited her lake-side house and land fifteen years ago and has lived there continuously.

Within the past year, the McKinneys moved in next-door to Johnson. Johnson was ill during their move, and sent her housekeeper to welcome the McKinneys to the neighborhood. Johnson heard from another Sudbury resident that the McKinneys were offended by the gesture because she did not greet them herself. The relationship between the McKinneys and Johnson has not since been repaired.

Three months ago, the McKinneys built a tennis court on their property. The McKinneys have repeatedly hit tennis balls into Johnson's garden and have damaged her flowers. After one such incident, Johnson yelled for the McKinneys to, "Keep your damn balls to yourself." Two nights after this verbal exchange, Johnson swam naked in the lake in front of her and the McKinneys' properties. The McKinneys turned on their flood lights while she was swimming and frightened Johnson. Johnson yelled at the McKinneys to "Turn [the lights] off, please! You're crude! You're a brute!" The McKinneys did not turn off their outdoors lights. Johnson ran across her lawn naked to her house. Johnson believes the McKinneys purposely illuminated the area to embarrass Johnson while she was not clothed outside.

Two days after the swimming incident, the McKinneys built a stockade fence on the property line separating the McKinneys' and Johnson's properties. The wooden fence spans the length of their land and blocks sunlight from reaching Johnson's garden. Johnson believes the McKinneys purposely constructed the fence to annoy her. Johnson is angry that her flowers are dying and she has asked us for our advice.

DISCUSSION

1.) The McKinneys' fence is likely not a private nuisance under the Massachusetts Spite Fence Statute because it is not unnecessarily high, was not maliciously erected and does not substantially violate Johnson's comfort in her estate.

Basic jurisprudence of property ownership entitles individuals the right to use their estate for personal enjoyment. Land-owners often exercise property rights by building fences to protect their lawn, or keep their children and pets within a safe boundary. The privilege of property is not unrestricted, but is qualified by the rights of adjoining neighbors. If a land-owner unreasonably infringes upon the property interest(s) of a neighbor, the court will award damages in a private nuisance suit. State legislatures have passed measures governing private nuisance suits involving fences. In Massachusetts, the legislature enacted the "Spite Fence Statute."

The Spite Fence Statute provides:

> A fence or other structure in the nature of a fence which unnecessarily exceeds six feet in height and is maliciously erected or maintained for the purpose of annoying the owners or occupants of adjoining property shall be deemed a private nuisance. Any such owner or occupant injured in the comfort or enjoyment of his estate thereby may have an action of tort for damages under chapter two hundred and forty-three.

MASS. GEN. LAWS ch. 49, § 21 (2012).

The policy behind the statute is balancing the interests of property-owners and their neighbors. Under the statute, four elements are required in order to establish that a particular fence is a private nuisance. The first element is the fence must exceed six feet in height. The second element is the fence must not be unnecessarily high. The third element is the fence must not be erected maliciously or maintained for the purpose of annoying a neighbor. The fourth element is the fence must not injure the comfort or enjoyment of a neighbor's estate.

There is no dispute that the McKinneys' fence is twelve feet high and thus the first element is satisfied. Because the remaining three elements are not clear on their face, I will review and analyze them for our purpose of deciding whether to present Johnson in her potential claim.

First, the McKinneys' fence likely does not unnecessarily exceed six feet because it was built to keep tennis balls out of Johnson's property and to prevent sight of Johnson swimming naked. Second, the fence was likely not maliciously erected because the McKinneys' intent behind building it was to prevent future altercations. Third, the fence does not substantially injure Johnson's comfort because the damages are minor. Because these three elements are not met, Johnson likely does not have a claim under the Spite Fence Statute and it is not in our best interest to represent her in this matter.

A. The McKinneys' fence likely does not unnecessarily exceed six feet in height because the fence's height serves a purpose in separating the neighbors.

Under the Massachusetts Spite Fence Statute, a fence is unlawful if "unnecessarily high." A fence is "unnecessarily" high when the gravity of the harm incurred by the neighbor outweighs the utility of the fence. *Rideout v. Knox*, 19 N.E. 390, 392 (Mass. 1889); *Rattigan v. Wile*, 841 N.E.2d 680 (Mass. 2006). In an early application of the Spite Fence Statue, the Massachusetts Supreme Judicial Court defined "unnecessarily" high. *Rideout*, 19 N.E. at 392. Rideout brought an action of tort against the Knox family for building a fence on their property-line solely to annoy Rideout. The court weighed the neighbors' interests and found the damages must be severe for the fence's height to be unnecessary. The court held that if a fence over six feet serves any purpose, then adjacent property-owners cannot claim damages, regardless of the motive to construct. *Id.*

In a more recent case, *Rattigan v. Wile*, the court expanded upon the *Rideout* scale to assess liability in a private nuisance claim. *Rattigan*, 841 N.E.2d at 687. Rattigan had been harassed by his adjacent neighbor, Wile, for several years. Wile constructed a fifteen foot white and yellow tent on the property-line and flew his helicopter over Rattigan's property in order to annoy Rattigan. The court found that the gravity of the harm caused to Rattigan outweighed the utility of Wile's conduct. *Id.* at 687. Because Wile acted maliciously, constructed without utility and substantially interfered with Rattigan's property interest, the court awarded Rattigan damages and an injunction against Wile. *Id.* at 691.

Unlike in Rattigan, the McKinneys' fence is likely not unnecessarily high because the structure has utility and its purpose outweighs Johnson's damages. The McKinneys' fence has significant function to prevent future arguments. The fence's height ensures tennis balls will not cross into Johnson's lawn, and will block the sight of Johnson swimming nude. Conversely, Johnson's ordinary comfort has not been substantially violated. Johnson's damages consist of her plants dying from the fence's shade imposed on her lawn. The court will likely not find the fence to be unnecessarily high because the height serves alternative purposes and does not substantially harm Johnson. Therefore the second condition of the Spite Fence Statute has not been satisfied.

B. The court will likely rule the McKinneys' fence was not maliciously erected because the McKinneys' dominant motive to construct was not malice.

The third condition courts consider under the Massachusetts Spite Fence Statute is whether the fence was maliciously erected or intended to annoy the adjacent neighbor. A fence is maliciously erected when malice is the dominant motive to build. *Rideout*, 19 N.E. at 393 (ruling not enough evidence existed to find the Knox family constructed the fence with the dominant motive of malice); *Rattigan*, 841 N.E.2d. at 691 (ruling Wile's primary intention was malice thus damages were awarded to Rattigan).

In applying the "dominant motive" rule to Johnson's case, the court will likely find the McKinneys did not primarily construct out of malice. Unlike in *Rideout*, several incidents occurred to prove the McKinneys' motive to construct. The arguments with Johnson over stray tennis balls and her swimming naked support the McKinneys in erecting a fence. As in *Rattigan*, the court can analyze the McKinneys' conduct to ascertain their motive to construct. The court will likely rule the McKinneys erected the fence not to annoy Johnson, as occurred in *Rattigan*, but to purposefully avert future conflict. *Rattigan*, 841 N.E.2d. at 690. The McKinneys' purpose to erect the fence was not malice because the fence serves to separate the neighbors; therefore the third element of the statute is not satisfied.

Alternatively, in other jurisdictions courts have ruled defendants can construct a fence if the plaintiff's behavior constitutes a private nuisance. *Healey v. Spaulding*, 71 A. 472, 473 (Me. 1908) (ruling the plaintiff continuously abused a neighbor; therefore the plaintiff's actions are a private nuisance and the defendant has a substantial cause to construct). Similar to Johnson's behavior, her yelling and nudity may substantiate the McKinneys' fence as a barrier against further infringement on the McKinneys property enjoyment. If the court analyzes the McKinneys' reason to construct either as dominantly motivated by malice, or as a means of protection, the court will likely hold the same order that the fence was not maliciously erected. In either approach, the third element of the Spite Fence Statute will likely not be satisfied.

C. Johnson's comfort and enjoyment of her estate were likely not injured enough to satisfy the Spite Fence Statute because her damages are minimal.

The fourth element of the statute entitles property-owners or occupants to enjoy their estate without injury to their comfort by neighbors. A fence must substantially interfere with ordinary comfort of property enjoyment or substantially decrease the use or value of the property in order for a court to award damages. *Rattigan*, 841 N.E.2d. at 686-687.

The Massachusetts court in *Rattigan* ascertained the injury to property comfort by reviewing the neighbor's conduct. The severity and length of harassment by Wile were a substantial infringement to Rattigan's property enjoyment and rental market value of his house. The court held unreasonable aesthetic conditions are sufficient for damages in a private nuisance suit. Furthermore, the court in *Rattigan* expanded upon this legal standard to award Rattigan with an injunction against Wile. The court ruled because Wile's same actions could have been achieved while diminishing Rattigan's harm, an injunction was valid to curtail future arguments between the neighbors.

Unlike in *Rattigan*, Johnson's injury and property value decrease were not substantial as a result of the McKinneys' actions. Johnson's damages consisted of dead plants as a result of shade created by the McKinneys' fence. The dead plants have likely not significantly decreased Johnson's property value. The court will likely not award damages for this type of infringement because Johnson's injury to her comfort of her property is minimal.

If Johnson seeks an injunction, the court will weigh the McKinneys' actions against Johnson's damages. First, if an injunction is granted, the McKinneys' fence, if shortened or removed, will not be effective in its purpose of separating the neighbors. Second, the burden on the McKinneys to deconstruct their fence outweighs Johnson's burden of moving her flowers. For the two reasons above and because Johnson's damages are minimal, the court is not likely to award an injunction against the McKinneys, therefore, I recommend that we should not represent Johnson as our client in this matter.

Other jurisdictions have not granted injunctions or damages in spite fence suits because courts have held the plaintiff's comfort in their estate has not been infringed. The right to a neighbor's air, light or view is an injury only when the interference was solely founded on malice. *Musumeci v. Leonardo*, 75 A.2d 175, 177-178 (R.I. 1950) (ruling the right to air and light is not enforceable because there is no injury under common law; therefore no relief granted); *Hornsby v. Smith*, 13 S.E.2d 20, 25 (Ga. 1941) (ruling the plaintiff did not prove the invasion of the right to air light was solely out of malice). The McKinneys' fence does not unlawfully obstruct Johnson's air, view and sunlight solely out of malice because the McKinneys' fence was not erected with the dominant motive of malice, see Section B *supra*. Johnson's claim of infringement under the Statute's fourth element is not an actionable injury because her comfort has not been substantially violated by significant damages.

CONCLUSION

We should not represent Johnson in this matter because she does not have a claim under the Massachusetts Spite Fence Statute as the McKinneys' fence (1) was not unnecessarily high, (2) was not maliciously erected and (3) did not cause substantial injury to Johnson's comfort in her property. First, the McKinneys' fence was not unnecessarily high because the utility of the fence outweighed Johnson's damages. Second, the McKinneys did not erect the fence with the dominant motive of malice because their intention was to avoid future altercations and to protect their property interest. Third, Johnson's damage to her plants is not substantial enough to interfere with her ordinary comfort of her property or rental market value and the obstruction of the McKinneys' air, light or view was not performed solely out of malicious. Given the probable absence of three out of four of the elements required under the Spite Fence Statute, Johnson likely does not have a claim for damages and I recommend that we do not represent her in this matter.

[F] SAMPLE LETTER OF INTENT

Dear China TelCom, Inc.,

This letter of intent sets forth our agreement as to the terms of the sale to the American Nexus Company (the "Buyer") by China TelCom, Inc. (the "Seller") of the Seller's business (the "Acquired Company"), located in Beijing, China and engaged in the telecommunications industry. By this agreement, the parties commence the negotiation of a binding and enforceable agreement (the "Acquisition" Agreement) for the purchase of the Acquired Company by the Seller to the Buyer. The execution of any Acquisition Agreement is subject to the satisfactory completion of Buyer's due diligence research of the Acquired Company. The parties agree to prepare and execute an Acquisition Agreement that will reflect the terms set forth in this letter of intent, and will contain customary representations and warranties.

It is proposed that the Acquisition Agreement include the following terms:

At the closing, the Purchaser will purchase all of the assets associated with the Acquired Company, including all current accounts, all outstanding contracts, all equipment, all intellectual property, and all documents, files and records regarding the operation of the Business.

The Buyer will assume as of the closing date only those obligations resultant from the operation of the Acquired Company after the closing date, and arising after the closing date in connection with the performance by the Buyer.

Purchase Price. The purchase price will be $300,000,000.00, payable via wire to be placed into an escrow account on the closing date.

The parties will inform all third parties with outstanding contracts relating to the operations of the Acquired Company of the potential sale and will use all reasonable efforts to acquire necessary third-party and government consents. The Seller will continue to operate the Acquired Company consistent with past performance. The Buyer and the Seller will be obligated to fulfill the obligations of the Acquisition Agreement, pending approval of all required signatures from third parties.

The Seller agrees to participate with the Buyer's due diligence investigation of the Acquired Company and to provide the Buyer and its representatives with immediate access to critical employees and to all records pertaining to the Acquired Company.

The Buyer will use the Due Diligence Information solely for the purpose of the Buyer's due diligence investigation of the Acquired Company. All information regarding the sale and purchase of the Acquired Company will be kept confidential, including any information prepared from the due diligence investigations. Buyer remains liable for any breach of confidentiality regarding the due dligence report or information on the sale and purchase of the Acquired Company. The provisions of this paragraph will survive the termination of this letter agreement.

Until May 30, 2011, the Seller will not enter into any agreement or discussion with any other corporation regarding the possible disposition of a material portion of the Acquired Company, or any business involving the telecommunications industry.

If the Acquired Company is not acquired by the Buyer, the Seller is unable to enforce the provisions of this letter of intent or the Acquisition Agreement, the Buyer will pay to the Seller a service fee equaling 1% of the purchase price, and the Seller's expenses in connection with the negotiation of the acquisition. All other, including legal fees, incurred in connection with the acquisition of the Acquired Company will be paid by each respective party.

If you are in agreement with the terms of this letter agreement, please execute this letter of intent and return a signed copy to our New York Office by the close of business on January 31, 2010. Upon receipt of a signed copy of this letter, we will proceed with negotiation and drafting of the Acquisition Agreement.

Sincerely,

American Nexus Company
By:______________________
[Name and Title]

____

China TelCom, Inc.
By: ______________________
[Name and Title]

[G] MODEL CORRESPONDENCE (LETTER)

November 27, 2011

Mr. Adam Smith
General Counsel
Drill Baby Drill, LLC
500 5th Avenue, Suite B
New York, NY 10036

Dear Mr. Smith,

It has come to our attention that you recently assigned a drilling contract that had been awarded to your company by the Colombian Department of Mines and Energy, to a Chinese firm. This is a violation of the non-assignment clause found in section 10.8 of our agreement, dated on June 14, 2010. Additionally, this may violate Colombian law and create liability for the Department of Labor.

As you know, your firm entered into an exclusive drilling contract with the Colombian Department of Mines and Energy on June 14, 2010. In that agreement, you were provided with the right to drill for oil and gas in the Soledad region of Colombia for a period not to exceed twelve months. As consideration for that agreement, the Colombian government would receive 10% of all net profits earned from the sale of any extracted commodities.

It has come to our attention that rather than arranging to drill in Soledad with your own labor and equipment, approximately one month after having signed the contract, you assigned your rights under this contract to a Chinese drilling company, which has since begun to drill off the coast of Soledad. As you are aware, the Colombian government already has contracts in place with public and private Chinese entities that provide licenses to drill in specific regions of the country. However, procurement regulations under Colombian law prohibit drilling licenses from being issued to any one country for more than 5% of Colombian territory. Combined with existing Chinese drilling contracts, your assignment provides drilling access to Chinese companies for over 5.4% of Colombian territory.

As a result of your actions, we are requesting a meeting with you in Bogotá, Colombia to discuss potential resolutions to this matter. Please note the urgency of this matter and make every effort to schedule a meeting with us promptly by contacting my office. Should the matter be left unresolved ten days from the date of this letter, we will have no choice but to terminate our contract and pursue damages against your firm. Thank you for your prompt attention to this matter.

Sincerely,

Juan Sanchez, Esq.

[H] MODEL CORRESPONDENCE (EMAIL)

Mr. Adam Smith
General Counsel
Drill Baby Drill, LLC
500 5th Avenue, Suite B
New York, NY 10036

Dear Mr. Smith,

I write to you on behalf of my client, the Colombian Department of Mines and Energy. Our office sent you a letter on April 5, 2011, requesting a meeting with you within ten days to avoid potential legal action against your company. As of the date of this email, you have not responded to that request.

As noted in the letter, the matter of your company's assignment of drilling rights in the Soledad region of Colombia to the Chinese firm Chu Wan Drilling is a violation of your Agreement with the Government of Colombia as well as a likely violation of Colombian law. Accordingly, our office has no choice but to pursue legal action against your company.

Our office has filed a claim with the Colombian Department of Justice against Drill Baby Drill, LLC, and also against Chu Wan Drilling. If you would like to discuss this matter further, please contact my office directly at 57.604.5527.

Sincerely,

Juan Sanchez, Esq.
General Counsel
Colombian Department of Mines

[I] SAMPLE DUE DILIGENCE REPORT

Mortgage Securitizations Ltd.
Due Diligence Report
Private and Confidential
January 2008

Contents

1. Summary and Findings
2. Legal Compliance
3. Conclusion and Recommendations

Summary and Findings

Please find below my analysis of the main areas of concern identified during the due diligence review conducted on Mortgage Securitizations Ltd. (the "company"):

(1.) Insufficient risk controls and preventative measures — the company has not enacted safety mechanisms or oversight control by management to prevent the sale of potential high-risk mortgages. Senior management does not review each mortgage that is sold into a package and thus does not identify any significant error that may occur through the sale of mortgages likely to default.

(2.) Overall structure of the company — As I did not receive any information from the company directly on its structure, I researched the company's organizational chart through its recent SEC filings. 11 board members control the company, and ownership interest is divided amongst shareholders. It remains unknown whether shareholders assume ownership and liability in the securitization of any high-risk mortgages. Additionally, the company provided me with inconsistent information regarding the date and state of incorporation of the company.

(3.) Weak Asset Management Systems — The most significant concern regarding the company's foundation is its weak systemization of the review of mortgages prior to buying and selling off the assets. All research, including potential risky investments, is entered into Microsoft Excel spreadsheets, which are then edited by several persons and never reviewed for a final assessment. To date, this system has not been scheduled for improvement or overhaul, which is necessary to ensure the company will not buy and sell faulty assets that could result in liability and/or major, devastating annual profit losses.

Legal Compliance

(1.) The company is following current market and real estate law; however, the risk the company is taking in buying potentially defaulted mortgages and then reselling through securitized packages may expose the company to future liability.

(2.) Within the company's 2006 and 2007 SEC filings, the company noted that it held assets in offshore accounts in Bermuda and Switzerland. I did not receive any information regarding this account from the senior management officials at the company. This issue would be worth investigating to determine any possible issues with legal compliance of domestic banking laws.

(3.) The company does not adequately inform buyers of the risk of acquiring securitized packages containing high-risk mortgages and thus suffers from poor transparency in its reporting. In addition, the company reported to me that it does not provide audited financial statements to its buyers, and would not forward the information to me for this due diligence report, thus limiting my ability to comment on any noted internal banking issues regarding the company.

Conclusion and Recommendations

(1.) In conducting a due diligence report, it is important to review the company for accurate and prompt reporting, consistency of information, quality answers for all questions, and transparency. In this review, the company did not provide full and complete answers to every inquiry posed. In addition, the company's officers provided inconsistent statements regarding foreign assets held in offshore accounts, alleging either there were none or "very few."

(2.) I recommend conducting a secondary due diligence review in order to supplement the current report. It will be necessary to review the company's foreign bank account assets and updated protocol for real estate portfolio management in order to fully determine the strength and mobility of the company going forward.

Appendix C:

DICTIONARY OF SELECT LEGAL TERMS

Abandonment: The voluntary surrender of property or rights.

Abatement: A decrease or reduction, often in price of rent or taxes due.

Abrogation: The act of superseding a former law by legislature or the courts.

Acceptance: Compliance with terms of a contract; or, taking an object in good faith.

Acquittal: To find, by authority of the court, a defendant not guilty.

Admonish: To caution against an unlawful act.

Adverse possession: The authorized taking of title to real property through fulfilling possession for a statutory period.

Affiant: Person who makes and signs an affidavit.

Allotment: Portion or division of the whole.

Annuity: Fixed, periodic payments over a certain time period.

Anticipatory breach of contract: Before satisfying all conditions of the contract, the promisor notifies the promisee that he cannot fully perform his duties under the contract.

Appearance: The act of coming into court as a party to the lawsuit.

Arbitration: The settling of a dispute through negotiations with an unbiased third-party.

Arrest of judgment: The act of staying a final order in a case by a judge because the judgment would be reversible if decided.

Asportation: The act of carrying away goods without legal authorization.

Assignment: To transfer property, real or personal, to another person or entity.

Assurance: A pledge or guaranty.

Attestation: To witness and sign a writing instrument.

Attorney-client privilege: The right of a client to refuse the disclosure of communication between the client and his attorney.

Aver: To declare or assert in argument.

Bad faith: To do an act dishonestly, not by negligence.

Bail: The posting of payment or surety to a court to allow the release of a defendant.

Bailment: The giving of goods or personal property by one person (bailor) to another person (bailee) by way of contract in trust of holding the goods or handle the goods as stated by the contract.

Balloon mortgage: A mortgage with specific payments paid at regular intervals with the final mortgage payment being significantly higher than any of the other payments.

Bankrupt: The condition of a person or entity unable to pay his debts either at the present time or as they become due.

Bequest: A gift of property by will.

Best evidence rule: The rule of evidence that prohibits the introduction of evidence into a case if the evidence is not the original document unless it is proven that the original document has been destroyed or is beyond the jurisdiction of the court by no fault of the party.

Bestow: To grant or give.

Bifurcated trial: The trying of issues separately in one case.

Bilateral contract: An agreement in which both parties are bound to fulfill their obligations in full to one another.

Binding agreement: A contract that is enforceable under law.

Black letter law: The principle or holding of law in a case application within a jurisdiction.

Boilerplate: Language used in a contract that has a standard meaning and is copied over for use without variation.

Bona fide: In good faith; actually or genuine.

Bond: A written obligation to repay a loan, often with a specified amount of interest for a specified time period.

Breach of contract: Failure, without legal reason, to complete part of or all conditions of a contract.

Broker: An agent who makes contracts on behalf of a buyer or seller for compensation.

Burden of proof: The duty of a party to prove evidence by an established degree of belief.

Cancellation: To terminate and make legally unenforceable.

Capitalization: The full amount of securities issued by a business., e.g., bonds, and stock.

Cash dividend: The amount of profits or surplus paid to stockholders by a corporation in the form of cash.

Cause of action: The facts that give a person the right to file for legal relief.

Circumstantial evidence: Facts not proven by first-hand knowledge but through deduction and inference.

Clear and convincing evidence: An intermediate standard of proof set in some cases depending on the issues and jurisdiction — more than a mere preponderance, but not as high as proof beyond a reasonable doubt.

Collateral: Property posted to be used as security to hold a debt.

Consideration: The motive or cause to enter into a contract.

Contingent: Conditioned upon another future event which is not certain to occur.

Conveyance: Transfer of title from seller to buyer by deed.

Covenant: An agreement between two or more people in writing, by which a party affirms to fulfill a duty to another party.

Damages: Compensation that is recoverable through a lawsuit in the courts to a person who has suffered injury.

Debtor: An entity or person who owes a debt.

Deed: A writing instrument in which a grantor transfers ownership of property.

Disposition: Transfer to the possession of another.

Domicile: The place of permanent residence.

Easement: The right to use of all or part of the property of another person.

Eminent domain: The taking of private property by the government for public use.

Equitable estoppel: The situation in which a person is prevented from changing his action against another who has justifiably relied upon and changed his position in reliance on the act of the other person.

Equitable relief: The type of damages awarded to a person in the form of an injunction or specific performance instead of money.

Estate: A person's amount of interest in real or personal property.

Exigent circumstances: Instance in which police officers may search a person, car or home without a warrant due to an emergency.

Ex post facto law: A law that is passed after an act occurs and is applied retroactively before the act occurred.

Fee: A fixed charge; property to be inherited without conditions attached.

Force majeure: Within an insurance contract, an unavoidable event that makes the contract unable to be performed.

Franchise: A license by an owner of property to another person to use and sell a trademarked item.

Fraud: The act of intentionally misrepresenting the truth to make another person rely and act on that lie.

Gift: A voluntary transfer of property to another person without conditions attached.

Grandfather clause: A clause in a new law that changes a previous law to allow persons already regulated by the previous law to continue to be regulated by the previous law.

Grant: To bestow or convey to another entity.

Gross income: All income from all sources before accounting for taxes and other payments.

Guaranty: A promise for the performance of an action to be done in a specific way by a guarantor, even if the principal obligor of the contract does not perform his duties.

Hearsay: An out-of-court statement entered into evidence for the truth of the matter asserted.

Indemnity: A contract in which one person is liable for financial loss to another.

Indictment: Formal writing written by the prosecution and presented before a grand jury charging a defendant with accused offense(s).

Injunction: Remedy issued by a court in which an action is prohibited from occurring.

Impeachment: The process in court of questioning the credibility of a witness through the use of evidence applied for this purpose.

Installment contract: Agreement in which party pays or performs periodically to other party.

Joinder: Uniting two or more persons in a legal proceeding.

Judicial Estoppel: The rule that parties are bound by judicial decisions and must act in accordance with those decisions.

Jurisdiction: The geographic or area of authority in which a court has the power to try a certain case.

Mandamus: Meaning "we command." Issued by a higher court to a lower court or entity directing action to be taken by the lower court or entity.

Negligence: The failure to perform an act that a reasonable and person would do under ordinary conditions.

Nonfeasance: Failing to fulfill an act that should have been performed.

Nuisance: An act of unreasonable or unlawful use of a person to his or her own property that infringes on the public or private interest of another.

Parol Evidence: Evidence given by word of mouth; with regard to contracts, the evidence is extraneous to the contract.

Peremptory challenge: The authority of a party in a lawsuit to dismiss a potential juror without reason (also called a "peremptory strike").

Plea bargaining: Process in which the parties negotiate the disposition of the case in reliance on order by court-approval.

Power of attorney: A duly-executed and signed written instrument permitting a person to act as another person's agent or attorney

Prejudice: Bias created by a forejudgment.

Preponderance of the evidence: Evidence weighed to establish it was more probably than not that the facts had occurred and therefore presented into evidence before the court.

Prima facie: A fact presumed to be true on the face of it in its initial entrance into evidence.

Probable cause: Having more evidence to prove the truth than not.

Promissory Estoppel: The situation in which a promise has been made and the promisor should reasonably expect to motivate the promisee to act, which does occur, and the promise is lawfully binding,

Promissory note: A promise in writing to pay a specific amount at a specific time to another person.

Quitclaim deed: A deed of conveyance that is set to release the title to another person without any warranties on the property.

Ratify: To make valid and confirm.

Rebuttable Evidence: The presumption that which may be rebutted by contrary evidence.

Rescission: The right to cancel a contract upon the occurrence of specific actions of default by the other party.

Satisfaction: The act of paying off all obligations to fulfill a debt between two parties.

Terms Sheet: A non-binding document that outlines the material terms and conditions of the agreement.

Writ of Certiorari: An order by the appellate-level court declaring whether the court will hear the pending case. If the court of appeals decides to hear the lower court case, then the case will be brought up to the court of appeals. If the court of appeals refuses to hear the case, then the lower court's decision stands.

INDEX

[References are to sections and appendices.]

A

ACADEMIC LEGAL WRITING
Generally . . . 7[A]
Article wrapping-up . . . 7[C][8]
Authorities validation . . . 7[C][7]
Case analyses . . . 7[B][1]
Issue papers . . . 7[B][2]
Manuscript, outline . . . 7[C][3]
Material with original writing, analyze . . . 7[C][5]
Original writing, analyze material with . . . 7[C][5]
Research plan development and execution . . . 7[C][4]
Research question, turning research topic into . . . 7[C][2]
Research topic formulation
  Generally . . . 7[C][1]
  Finding topic . . . 7[C][1][a]
Stages of
  Generally . . . 7[C]
  Article wrapping-up . . . 7[C][8]
  Authorities validation . . . 7[C][7]
  Manuscript, outline . . . 7[C][3]
  Material with original writing, analyze . . . 7[C][5]
  Original writing, analyze material with . . . 7[C][5]
  Research plan development and execution . . . 7[C][4]
  Research question, turning research topic into . . . 7[C][2]
  Research topic formulation
    Generally . . . 7[C][1]
    Finding topic . . . 7[C][1][a]
  Transitions and headings, connect thoughts with . . . 7[C][6]
Transitions and headings, connect thoughts with . . . 7[C][6]
Types of
  Generally . . . 7[B]
  Case analyses . . . 7[B][1]
  Issue papers . . . 7[B][2]

AMBIGUOUS DRAFTING
Generally . . . 3[H]
Exercise solutions . . . App.A[A]

C

CASE BRIEFS DRAFTING
Generally . . . 5[A]; 5[D]
Analysis . . . 5[D][7]
Case citation . . . 5[D][1]
Decision . . . 5[D][4]
Facts . . . 5[D][2]
Holding of the court . . . 5[D][4]
Issues . . . 5[D][3]

CASE BRIEFS DRAFTING—Cont.
Opinions, separate . . . 5[D][6]
Parties . . . 5[D][1]
Procedural history . . . 5[D][2]
Reasoning . . . 5[D][5]
Sample case briefs . . . App.B[C], [D]

CLIENT ADVICE LETTER
Correspondence drafting . . . 4[C]

CONTRACT DRAFTING
Generally . . . 6[A]
Attachments . . . 6[G][2]
Back of contract
  Generally . . . 6[G]
  Attachments . . . 6[G][2]
  Exhibits . . . 6[G][2]
  Schedules . . . 6[G][2]
  Signature page . . . 6[G][1]
Body of contract
  Boilerplate clauses . . . 6[F][14]
  Choice of forum . . . 6[F][1]; 6[F][2][b]
  Choice of law clause . . . 6[F][1]; 6[F][2][a]
  Counterparts . . . 6[F][13]
  Defined terms . . . 6[F][1]
  Disclaimer clause . . . 6[F][4]
  Force majeure clause . . . 6[F][11]
  Forum non conveniens . . . 6[F][1]; 6[F][2][c]
  Indemnification clause . . . 6[F][5]
  Liquidated damages clause . . . 6[F][7]
  Merger clause . . . 6[F][6]
  Notice clause . . . 6[F][10]
  Representations and warranties clause . . . 6[F][3]
  Saving clause . . . 6[F][9]
  Severability clause . . . 6[F][9]
  Term and termination clause . . . 6[F][8]
  Waiver clause . . . 6[F][12]
Boilerplate clauses . . . 6[F][14]
Choice of forum . . . 6[F][1]; 6[F][2][b]
Choice of law clause . . . 6[F][1]; 6[F][2][a]
Counterparts . . . 6[F][13]
Defined terms . . . 6[F][1]
Disclaimer clause . . . 6[F][4]
Discretion, language of . . . 6[D][1]
Drafting pointers
  Currency
    Numbers and . . . 6[H][1]
    Tips on drafting . . . 6[H][3]
  Numbers
    Generally . . . 6[H][4]
    Currency, and . . . 6[H][1]
  Time of day, tips on drafting . . . 6[H][2]
  Tips on drafting
    Currency . . . 6[H][3]
    Time of day . . . 6[H][2]
Effective contract drafting skills, importance of . . . 6[B]

[References are to sections and appendices.]

CONTRACT DRAFTING—Cont.
Exhibits . . . 6[G][2]
Force majeure clause . . . 6[F][11]
Forum non conveniens . . . 6[F][1]; 6[F][2][c]
Front of contract
 Generally . . . 6[E]
 Contract title . . . 6[E][1]
 Introductory clause . . . 6[E][1]
 Recitals . . . 6[E][2]
 Title . . . 6[E][1]
Indemnification clause . . . 6[F][5]
Introductory clause . . . 6[E][1]
Language, types of
 Generally . . . 6[D]
 Discretion, language of . . . 6[D][1]
 Obligation, language of . . . 6[D][1]
Letters of intent . . . 6[C]
Liquidated damages clause . . . 6[F][7]
Merger clause . . . 6[F][6]
Notice clause . . . 6[F][10]
Obligation, language of . . . 6[D][1]
Oral contracts vs written contracts . . . 6[I]
Parol evidence . . . 6[K]
Promissory estoppel and reliance . . . 6[J]
Recitals . . . 6[E][2]
Reliance, promissory estoppel and . . . 6[J]
Representations and warranties clause . . . 6[F][3]
Saving clause . . . 6[F][9]
Schedules . . . 6[G][2]
Severability clause . . . 6[F][9]
Signature page . . . 6[G][1]
Term and termination clause . . . 6[F][8]
Title, contract . . . 6[E][1]
Waiver clause . . . 6[F][12]
Written contracts vs oral contracts . . . 6[I]

CORRESPONDENCE DRAFTING
Generally . . . 4[A]; 4[B]
Client advice letter . . . 4[C]
Email communications . . . 4[D]
Technology tips
 Generally . . . 4[E]; 4[F]
 Custom auto-signatures, setting . . . 4[E][3]
 Message delivery, delaying . . . 4[E][1]
 Read notification, requesting . . . 4[E][2]
 Return receipt, requesting . . . 4[E][2]

CUSTOM AUTO-SIGNATURES
Correspondence drafting . . . 4[E][3]

D

DEMAND LETTER
Sample . . . App.B[B]

DICTIONARY OF LEGAL TERMS
Generally . . . App.C

DISCLAIMER CLAUSE
Contract drafting . . . 6[F][4]

DOCUMENTS
Foreign legal practitioners, legal documents for . . . 2[C]
Sample (See SAMPLE DOCUMENTS)

DRAFT EDITING AND FINALIZING
Generally . . . 9[A]
Grammar and style editing . . . 9[B]
Style editing, grammar and . . . 9[B]
Substantive editing . . . 9[C]

DRAFTING
Ambiguous drafting and word choice
 Generally . . . 3[H]
 Exercise solutions . . . App.A[A]
Case briefs (See CASE BRIEFS DRAFTING)
Contract (See CONTRACT DRAFTING)
Correspondence (See CORRESPONDENCE DRAFTING)
Draft editing and finalizing (See DRAFT EDITING AND FINALIZING)
Legal memorandum (See LEGAL MEMORANDUM DRAFTING)

DUE DILIGENCE REPORT
Sample . . . App.B[I]

E

EMAIL
Correspondence drafting . . . 4[D]
Model correspondence . . . App.B[H]

EXHIBITS
Contract drafting . . . 6[G][2]

F

FORCE MAJEURE CLAUSE
Contract drafting . . . 6[F][11]

FORUM NON CONVENIENS
Contract drafting . . . 6[F][1]; 6[F][2][c]

FRAMING THE ISSUE EXERCISE
Generally . . . 5[B][6]
Solutions . . . App.A[F]

I

INDEMNIFICATION CLAUSE
Contract drafting . . . 6[F][5]

L

LANGUAGE
Contract drafting, types in (See CONTRACT DRAFTING, subhead: Language, types of)
Superfluous language
 Generally . . . 3[C]
 Exercise solutions . . . App.A[B]

[References are to sections and appendices.]

LEGAL CITATION
Generally . . . 8[A]
Importance of . . . 8[B]
Technology and citation . . . 8[C]

LEGAL MEMORANDUM DRAFTING
Generally . . . 5[A]; 5[B]
Answer, short . . . 5[B][3]
Closing thoughts on . . . 5[C]
Conclusion . . . 5[B][6]
Discussion . . . 5[B][5]
Facts, statement of . . . 5[B][4]
Framing the issue exercise . . . 5[B][6]; App.A[F]
Headings . . . 5[B][1]
Question presented . . . 5[B][2]
Recommendations . . . 5[B][6]
Short answer . . . 5[B][3]
Sources of law exercise . . . 5[B][6]; App.A[G]
Statement of facts . . . 5[B][4]

LEGAL TERMS
Dictionary of select . . . App.C

LEGAL WRITING, EFFECTIVE
Generally . . . 3[A]; Ch.1; Ch.10
Academic legal writing (See ACADEMIC LEGAL WRITING)
Acronyms . . . 3[L][4]
Ambiguous drafting and word choice
 Generally . . . 3[H]
 Exercise solutions . . . App.A[A]
American legal writing, unique qualities of
 Generally . . . 2[B]
 Brevity, demand for . . . 2[B][1]
 Issue identification, clear . . . 2[B][3]
 Plain legal English . . . 2[B][2]
 Succinct conclusions . . . 2[B][4]
Capitalization . . . 3[L][3]
Clear sentences . . . 3[E]
Final pointers
 Acronyms . . . 3[L][4]
 Capitalization . . . 3[L][3]
 Punctuation . . . 3[L][1]
 Spacing . . . 3[L][2]
Foreign legal practitioners, importance of effective legal writing for
 American legal writing, unique qualities of (See subhead: American legal writing, unique qualities of)
 Legal documents . . . 2[C]
 Risks of ineffective legal writing . . . 2[A]
Legal style, review . . . 3[K]
Paragraph structure, sentence sequencing and . . . 3[G]
Parallel structure
 Generally . . . 3[I]
 Exercise solutions . . . App.A[D]
Punctuation . . . 3[L][1]
Sentences
 Sequencing and paragraph structure . . . 3[G]
 Structure . . . 3[D]
Spacing . . . 3[L][2]

LEGAL WRITING, EFFECTIVE—Cont.
Superfluous language
 Generally . . . 3[C]
 Exercise solutions . . . App.A[B]
Transitions . . . 3[F]
Voice
 Generally . . . 3[J]
 Exercise solutions . . . App.A[E]
Word choice
 Generally . . . 3[B]
 Ambiguous drafting and
  Generally . . . 3[H]
  Exercise solutions . . . App.A[A]

LETTERS
Client advice letter . . . 4[C]
Demand letter sample . . . App.B[B]
Letter of intent
 Contract drafting . . . 6[C]
 Editing; exercise . . . App.A[H]
 Sample . . . App.B[F]
Model correspondence . . . App.B[G]
Opinion letter sample . . . App.B[A]

LIQUIDATED DAMAGES CLAUSE
Contract drafting . . . 6[F][7]

M

MEMORANDUM
Legal memorandum drafting (See LEGAL MEMORANDUM DRAFTING)
Office memorandum; sample . . . App.B[E]

MERGER CLAUSE
Contract drafting . . . 6[F][6]

N

NOTICE CLAUSE
Contract drafting . . . 6[F][10]

O

OFFICE MEMORANDUM
Sample . . . App.B[E]

OPINION LETTER
Sample . . . App.B[A]

ORAL CONTRACTS
Written contracts compared . . . 6[I]

P

PARALLEL STRUCTURE
Effective legal writing and
 Generally . . . 3[I]
 Exercise solutions . . . App.A[D]

PAROL EVIDENCE
Contract drafting . . . 6[K]

[References are to sections and appendices.]

PROMISSORY ESTOPPEL
Contract drafting . . . 6[J]

R

RELIANCE
Contract drafting . . . 6[J]

REPRESENTATIONS AND WARRANTIES CLAUSE
Contract drafting . . . 6[F][3]

S

SAMPLE DOCUMENTS
Case briefs . . . App.B[C], [D]
Demand letter . . . App.B[B]
Due diligence report . . . App.B[I]
Letter of intent; sample . . . App.B[F]
Model correspondence
  Email . . . App.B[H]
  Letter . . . App.B[G]
Office memorandum . . . App.B[E]
Opinion letter . . . App.B[A]

SAVING CLAUSE
Contract drafting . . . 6[F][9]

SENTENCES
Clear . . . 3[E]
Sequencing and paragraph structure . . . 3[G]
Structure
  Generally . . . 3[D]
  Exercise solutions . . . App.A[C]

SEVERABILITY CLAUSE
Contract drafting . . . 6[F][9]

SIGNATURE PAGE
Contract drafting . . . 6[G][1]

SOURCES OF LAW EXERCISE
Generally . . . 5[B][6]
Solutions . . . App.A[G]

SUPERFLUOUS LANGUAGE
Exercise solutions . . . App.A[B]
Writing, effective . . . 3[C]

T

TERM AND TERMINATION CLAUSE
Contract drafting . . . 6[F][8]

V

VOICE
Generally . . . 3[J]
Exercise solutions . . . App.A[E]

W

WAIVER CLAUSE
Contract drafting . . . 6[F][12]

WORD CHOICE
Ambiguous drafting and
  Generally . . . 3[H]
  Exercise solutions . . . App.A[A]
Legal writing, effective . . . 3[B]